AF131138

APHRAATES AND THE JEWS

CONTRIBUTIONS TO ORIENTAL HISTORY AND PHILOLOGY
VOL. IX

APHRAATES AND THE JEWS

A STUDY
OF THE CONTROVERSIAL HOMILIES OF THE
PERSIAN SAGE IN THEIR RELATION TO
JEWISH THOUGHT

BY

FRANK GAVIN

———

AMS PRESS INC.
New York
1966

AMS PRESS, INC.
New York, N.Y. 10003
1966

CONJUGI
CARISSIMAE

NOTE

THE Early Syriac writer called Aphraates, who lived in the fourth century of our Era and was Bishop of the Convent of Mār Matthew near to Mosul, has left us some homilies which have been of interest to the students of Christian theology from a time antedating even their appearance in the language in which they were written. Since their publication in Syriac by the late William Wright in 1869, they have preserved their old-time consideration. In the following study, the Rev. Dr. Gavin has endeavoured to find the proper background for a number of these homilies — especially for those dealing with the Jews. He has shown — I think with success — how the Persian Sage, in combatting his theological opponents, has become indebted to them for much of his method and for many of his examples; though, as is natural, using both for his own purposes. Dr. Gavin is careful and sure-footed in his investigations; and I commend his study to the attention of those modern "wise men," who are interested in knowing about the early history of the Christian Church.

Columbia University, New York
March 10, 1922.

RICHARD GOTTHEIL.

TABLE OF CONTENTS

BIBLIOGRAPHY

I. Editions of the Text.

1. Wright, William, *The Homilies of Aphraates,*[1] *the Persian Sage, edited from Syriac Manuscripts of the fifth and sixth centuries, in the British Museum, with an English Translation,* vol. I, *The Syriac Text,* London, 1869.[2]
2. Parisot, John,[3] *Aphraatis Sapientis Persae Demonstrationes,* in *Patrologia Syriaca, accurante R. Graffin, Pars Prima (ab initiis usque ad annum 350): Tomus primus,* Paris, 1894, and *tomus secundus,* cols. 1—489, Paris, 1907.

II. Translations of the text (complete, or in part).

3. Antonelli, H., *S. Jacobi Nisibeni Opera Omnia ex Armeno in Latinum Sermonem Translata,* Rome, 1756; later reprinted (lacking, however, some of Antonelli's notes) in Gallandius, *Bibliotheca Veterum Patrum,* vol. V, pp. 3—164,—containing Homilies I—XIX, inclusive.
4. Bert, G., *Aphraat's des persischen Weisen Homilien, aus dem Syrischen übersetzt und erläutert,* in *Texte und Untersuchungen,* (Gebhardt und Harnack) *Band III, Heft 3 und 4,* Leipzig, 1888[4].

---

[1] In his *Short History of Syriac Literature,* Wright gives (pp. 32—33) a summary of the evidence regarding Aphraates, from George, Bishop of the Arab tribes (714), through Elias (11th. cent.), Bar-Hebraeus (13th cent.), and Abhd-Isho (14th cent.). In the *Histoire Nestorienne, Chronique de Seert,* (dated 13th cent., according to Scher, p. 217) edited by Scher in the *Patrologia Orientalis, tome IV, fascicule 3,* Paris, 1907, p. 292, and the 'Kitab al-Unwan', or *Histoire Universelle, ecrite par Agapius de Menbij,* edited by Vasielief, tome VII, fasc. 4, p. 566, Aphraates is called الحكيم الفارسى and افراهاط الحكيم الفارسى. The translation of the former passage (*P. O.,* t. IV, p. 292) by *le medicin persan* is not accurate, as it represents the Syriac: ܐܡܝܕܐ ܚܟܝܡܐ ܗܕܝܢܐ, as in, *e. g.* Elias b. Shinaya.

[2] This is the *editio princeps,* and the promised English translation never appeared. The notes (pp. 1—39, 42—63) are extremely valuable. For an excellent review, cf. that of Nöldeke, in *Götting. gelehrt. Anz.* 1869, pp. 1521—1532.

[3] Dom Parisot's notes are of the greatest value, (pp. i—lxxx), as are his lexicon, index, and concordance (2nd vol., cols. 151—489).

[4] Reviewed by Wellhausen, in *Theol. Litter. Zeitung,* 1889, pp. 77 ff., and Bonwetsch, in *Theol. Litt. Blätter,* 1889, pp. 267 ff.

5. Bickell, G., *Ausgewählte Schriften syrischer Kirchenväter*, — *Aphra-ates, Rabulas, und Isaac von Nineveh*, in Thalhofer, *Bibliothek der Kirchenväter*, Kempten, 1874, — containing Homilies I—IV, VII, VIII, XII, XVIII and XXII, in German translation.
6. Budge, W., *The Discourses of Philoxenus of Mabbug*, vol. II, London, 1894, — English translation of Homily I, pp. clxxxv, ff.
7. Forget, J., *De Vita et Scriptis Aphraatis Sapientis Persae*, Louvain, 1882, — Latin translation of Homily XXI, pp. 330—353.
8. Gwynn, J., *Select Demonstrations of Aphrahat*, in *Nicene and Post-Nicene Fathers, second series*, vol. XIII, Christian Literature Association, (N. Y.) 1898, — English translation of Homilies I, V, VI, VIII, X, XVII, XXI and XXII, pp. 345—412.

III. Introduction to the *Homilies*, articles, and monographs on Aphraates.[1]

9. Forget, J., *De Vita et Scriptis Aphraatis Sapientis Persae, disser-tatio historico-theologica*, Louvain, 1882.
10. Hartwig, E., *Untersuchungen sur Syntax des Afraatis, I, Die Relativpartikel und der Relativsatz*, Leipzig, 1893.
11. Ryssel, G., *Ein Brief Georgs, Bischof der Araber*, Gotha, 1883.
12. Sasse, C. J. F., *Prolegomena in Aphraatis Sapientis Persae Sermones Homileticos*, Leipzig, 1878.
    (Reviewed by Bardenhewer, in *ZKTh.*, 1879, pp. 369—378.)
13. Schwen, P., *Untersuchungen über den persischen Weisen*, Berlin, 1907; (excellent bibliography, pp. 7—9). Also *s. v*, *Afrahat, Seine Person und seine Verständniss des Christentums; ein Beitrag sur Geschichte der Kirche im Osten*, ed. Bonwetsch, (Berlin) 1907.
14. Schönfelder, *Aus und über Aphraates*, in *Tübinger Abhandlung Quartalschrift* 1878, pp. 195—256.
    (Reviewed by Bardenhewer, *ZKTh.*, vol. III, pp. 373 and notes.)

IV. Brief notes, articles, and incidental references to Aphraates, embodying information of value as to the interpretation of his work.

15. Albert, F. X. E., *s. v.*, "Aphraates", in the *Catholic Encyclopedia*, New York, 1907, vol. I, pp. 593—594.
16. Bardenhewer, *Patrologie*, 2nd ed., Freiburg i. B., 1901, pp. 338—340.
17. Braun, O., *Moses bar Kepha und sein Buch von der Seele*, Frei-burg i. B., 1891, note 12, p. 137; note 18, pp. 142—148.

[1] Cf. also, Kittel, G., *Eine synagogale Parallele zu den Benai Q'jâmâ*, in *ZNTW* 1915, vol. XVI, pp. 235—236.
Plooij, D., *Der descensus ad inferos in Aphrahat und den Oden Salomos*, in *ZNTW*, 1913, vol. XIV, pp. 222—231.

Cf. also, his *Beiträge zur Geschichte der Eschatologie in den syrischen Kirchen, ZKTh.*, 1892, vol. XVI, pp. 272—317.

18. Burkitt, F. C., *Aphraates and Monasticism, a Reply*, in the *Journal of Theological Studies*, vol. VIII, pp. 10—15. (cf. *s. v. Connolly* below).

19. Burkitt, F. C., *Early Christianity outside the Roman Empire*, Cambridge, 1899.

20. Burkitt, F. C., *Early Eastern Christianity, the St. Margaret's Lectures, 1904, on the Syriac-speaking Church*, New York, 1904.

21. Connolly, R. H., *Aphraates and Monasticism*, in *JThS.*, vol. VI, 1904—1905, pp. 286—290; 522—539.

22. Connolly, R. H., *The Creed of Aphraates*, in *ZNTW*, vol. VII, 1906, pp. 204 ff; and in *JThS.*, vol. IX, pp. 572—576, (in answer to Pass' article.)

23. Connolly, R. H., *St. Ephraim and Encratism*, in *JThS*, vol. VIII, pp. 41—48.

24. Harnack, A., *Dogmengeschichte, s. v. "Aphraates", passim.*

25. Labourt, J., *Le christianisme dans l'Empire perse, sous la dynastie sassanide, 224—632*, Paris, 1904.
    (Cf. s. v. "Afraat", especially pp. 28—42, 47—50. Reviewed in *Révue des Etudes juives*, vol. L, p. 278.)

26. Loofs, F., *Leitfaden der Dogmengeschichte*, 4th ed., 1906, *s. v.*, "Aphraates".

27. Nestlè, E., in *Realencyclopedia für protestantische Theologie und Kirche*, Leipzig, 1896, vol. I, p. 611.

28. Pass, H. L., *The Creed of Aphraates*, in *JThS.*, vol. IX, pp. 267—284. (Cf. above, *s. v. Connolly* and *Burkitt.*)

29. Seeberg, R., *Lehrbuch der Dogmengeschichte*, Leipzig, 1905, *s. v.*, "Aphraates".

30. Weingarten, in Herzog's *Realencyclopaedie*, 2nd ed., vol. X, *s. v.*, "Mönchtum", pp. 758—792.

31. Wigram, W. A., in Murray's *Dictionary of Christian Biography*, *s. v.* "Aphraat", pp. 31—32.

32. Zahn, Th., *Forschungen zur Geschichte des N. T.-lichen Kanons und der altkirchlichen Literatur*, Erlangen, 1882—1884; vol. I, pp. 72—79; 376; vol. II, pp. 188, n. 5, 281—285; vol. III, pp. 275 et al.
    (The brief notes on Aphraates in the standard histories of Syriac literature, such as those of William Wright (*A Short History of Syriac Literature*, London, 1894, pp. 4, 9, 32—33, 143, etc.) and Rubens Duval (*La littérature syriaque*, Paris, 1900, pp. 224—229, etc.) contain nothing of very great significance).

V. Special studies on the relation of Aphraates to Jewish thought.

33. Funk, S., *Die haggadischen Elemente in den Homilien des Aphraates, des persischen Weisen*, Vienna, 1891.

34. Ginzberg, L., in the *Jewish Encyclopedia, s. v. "Aphraates"*, vol. XII, pp. 663—665.

35. Ginzberg, L., *Die Haggada bei den Kirchenväter und in der apokryphischen Litteratur*, Berlin 1900.
   (Cf. also the article *Die Kirchenvätern in ihrem Verhältniss zur talmudisch-midraschischen Litteratur, insbesondere zur Haggada*, in *Königsbergers Monatsblätter für Vergangenheit und Gegenwart des Judenthums*, Berlin, 1890—1891, vol. I, *Heft* 1—4.)

VI. Works used in the study of Aphraates' affiliations with Judaism

Adler, Michael, *The Emperor Julian and the Jews*, in *Jewish Quarterly Review*, Vol. V, (old style) 1892—1893, pp. 591—651.

Bacher, Wilhelm, *Die Agada der babylonischen Amoräer*, Strassburg i. E., 1878.

Bacher, Wilhelm, *Le mot 'Minim' dans le Talmud, designe-t-il quelquefois des chrétiens?* in *Révue des Études juives*, vol. XXXVIII, 1899, pp. 38—46.

Bacher, Wilhelm, *Rome dans le Talmud et le Midrasch*, in *Révue des Études juives*, vol. XXXIII, 1896, pp. 187—196.

Berliner, A., *Beiträge zur Geographie und Ethnographie Babyloniens im Talmud und Midrasch*, in *Jahresbericht des Rabbiner-Seminars zu Berlin pro 5643*, (Berlin, 1884).

Bethune-Baker, J., *Nestorius and his Teaching*, Cambridge, 1908, cf. appendix on the history of the Syriac terms 'ithutha' etc., pp. 217—232.

Bewer, J., *The History of the New Testament Canon in the Syriac Church*, in *The American Journal of Theology*, 1900, pp. 64 ff.

Bischoff, E., *Jesus und die Rabbinen*, Leipzig, 1905.

Bousset, Wilhelm, *Die Religion des Judenthums im neutestamentlichen Zeitalter*, Berlin, 1903.

Brüll, N., *Die Entstehungsgeschichte des babylonischen Thalmuds als Schriftwerks*, in *Jahrbuch für jüdische Geschichte und Litteratur*, vol. II, 1876, Frankfort a. M., pp. 1—123.

Buber, S., *Pesikta de-Rab Kahana*, Lyck, 1868.

Cohen, H., *Der heilige Geist*, in *Festschrift zum 70ten Geburtstag J. Guttmanns*, Leipzig, 1915, pp. 1—21.

Elbogen, J., *Studien zur Geschichte des jüdischen Gottesdienstes*, Berlin, 1907.

Enelow, H. G., *Kewwana; the Struggle for Inwardness in Judaism*, in *Studies in Jewish Literature, in honor of K. Kohler*, Berlin, 1913. pp. 83—107.

Franck, Ad., *Le péché originel et la femme*, in *Actes et Conferences de la Société des Études juives*, Paris, 1886, vol. I, pp. 5—19.

Frey, J., *Tod, Seelenglaube, und Seelenkult*, Leipzig, 1898.

Friedländer, M., *Patristische und talmudische Studien*, Vienna, 1878.

Friedmann, M., (ed.) *Mekilta*, Vienna, 1870.

Friedmann, M., *Sifre debé Rab*, Vienna, 1864.

Funk, S., *Das litterarische Leben der babylonischen Juden im 4ten Jahrhundert*, in *MGWJ*, 1906, pp. 385—405.

Funk, S., *Die Juden in Babylonien* (200—500), vol. I, under Sapor I, Berlin, 1902; vol. II, under Sapor II, in *MGWJ*, 1905, pp. 534—566.

Goldfahn, A., *Die Kirchenväter und die Agada*, Breslau, 1889.

Graetz, H., *Volkstümliche Geschichte der Juden*, vols. I—III, Leipzig, 1888.

Halevy, I., דורות הראישונים, vol. II, Frankfurt a. M., 1901; vol. III Pressburg, 1898.

Hamburger, J., *Real-Encyclopädie für Bibel und Talmud, Abtheilung II, die Talmudischen Artikel A—Z*, Strelitz, 1882, supplementary volume I, Leipzig, 1886.

Harnack, A., *Judenthum und Judenchristen in Justins Dialog mit Trypho*, in *T. u. U., 3. Reihe, 9. Band*, (vol. XXXIX) Leipzig, 1913, pp. 47—98.

Harris, J. Rendel, *The Teaching of the Apostles and the Sibylline Books*, Cambridge, 1885.

Heilprin, S., ספר סדר הדורות, Warsaw, 1878.

Herford, R. T., *Christianity in Talmud and Midrash*, London, 1903.

Hershon, I., חמשה חומשי תורה לפי התלמוד, London, 1870.

Hirschensohn, I. T., ספר שבע חכמות, Lemberg, 1883 and London, 1912.

Hyman, A., תולדות תנאים ואמורים, London, 1910.

Judelwitz, P., חיי היהודים בזמן התלמוד ספר נהרדעא, Wilna, 1905.

Klein, G., *Zu Erläuterung der Evangelien aus Talmud und Midrasch*, in *ZNTW*, vol. V, 1914, pp. 144—153.

Kmosko, M., *Simeon bar Sabba'e*, in *Patrologia Syriaca*, ed R. Graffin, *pars prima, tomus secundus*, Paris, 1907, cols. et pp. 60—1055.

Kohler, K., *Jewish Theology*, New York, 1918.

Krauss, S., *Das Leben Jesu nach jüdischen Quellen*, Berlin, 1902.

Laible, H., *Jesus Christus im Talmud*, Leipzig, 1900.

Lazarus, F., *Die Häupter der Vertriebenen*, רישי גלותא *Beiträge zu einer Geschichte der Exilsfürsten in Babylonien unter den Arsakiden und Sassaniden*, Frankfort a. M., 1890, (and in *Jahrbücher für jüdische Geschichte und Literatur*, vol. X., 1890):

Lazarus, M., *Die Ethik des Judenthums*, Frankfort, 1898.

Lévi, I., *Le péché originel dans les anciennes sources juives*, Paris, 1909.

Lock, W., and Sanday, W., *Two Lectures on the Sayings of Jesus*, Oxford, 1897.

Marmorstein, A., *The Doctrine of Merits in Old Rabbinical Literature*, (publication no. 7 of the Jews' College), London, 1920.

Mielziner, M., *Introduction to the Talmud*, New York, 1903.

Montefiore, C. G., *Rabbinic Conceptions of Repentance*, in *Jewish Quarterly Review*, 1904, pp. 209—257.

Moore, G. F., *The Last Adam, Alleged Jewish Parallels*, in 'Biblical Notes', *JBL*, vol. XVI, 1897, pp. 158—161.

Neubauer, Ad., *La geographie du Talmud*, Paris, 1868.

Nöldeke, Th., *Geschichte der Perser und Araber zur Zeit der Sassaniden, aus der arabischen Kronik des Tabari übersetzt*, Leyden, 1879.

Pirot, L., *L'oeuvre exégétique de Théodore de Mopsueste*, Rome, 1913.

Porter, F. C., *The Pre-existence of the Soul in the Book of Wisdom and in the Rabbinic Writings*, in the *American Journal of Theology*, vol. XII, 1908, no. 1, pp. 53—115.

Porter, F. C., *The Yeçer Hara*, in *Yale Biblical and Semitic Studies*, pp. 91—156.

Resch, *Agrapha*, in *T. u. U.*, Band V, Heft 4 ff., Leipzig, 1889.

Rosen, P., *Midrasch Tanchuma*, Warsaw, 1892.

Saphir, A., *Christus und die Schrift*, Leipzig, 1894.

Schechter, S., *Some Aspects of Rabbinic Theology*, New York, 1909.

Schechter, S., *Some Rabbinic Parallels to the New Testament*, in *Jewish Quarterly Review*, vol. XII, 1900, pp. 415—433.

Schechter, S., (ed.) *Aboth de Rabbi Nathan*, London, 1887.

Schiele, F., *Die rabbinischen Parallelen su 1 Kor.*, *XV*, 45—50, in *ZWT*, 1899, pp. 10—35.

Spira, S., *Die Eschatologie der Juden nach Talmud und Midrasch*, Halle, 1889.

Strack, H., *Einleitung in den Talmud*, Leipzig, 1908.

Strack, H., *Jesus, die Häretiker, und die Christen*, Leipzig, 1910.

Taylor, C., *Essay on the Theology of the Didache*, Cambridge, 1889.

Taylor, C., *The Oxhyrhynchus Logia and the Apocryphal Gospels*, Oxford, 1889.

Taylor, C., *The Oxhyrhnychus Sayings found in 1903*, Oxford, 1905.

Taylor, C., *The Teaching of the Twelve Apostles*, Oxford, 1886.

Teichmann, E., *Die paulinischen Vorstellungen von Auferstehung und Gericht, und ihre Beziehung sur jüdischen Apokalyptik*, Freiburg i. B., 1896.

Ter-Minassiantz, Erwand, *Die armenische Kirche in ihren Beziehungen su den syrischen Kirchen, bis sum Ende des 13. Jahrhunderts, nach den armenischen und syrischen Quellen bearbeitet*, in *T. u. U.*, vol. XII (*neuer Folge*), Heft 4, pp. 12—212, Leipzig, 1904.

Unna, I., *Babylonien um das Ende der Tannaitenzeit*, in *Jahrbuch d. Jüdischen Litteratur-Gesellschaft*, I, pp. 269—277, 1903.

Volz, P., *Der Geist Gottes*, Tübingen, 1910.

Weber, F., *Jüdische Theologie auf Grund des Talmuds und verwandter Schriften dargestellt*, Leipzig, 1897.

Weiss, I. H., *Mekilta de Rabbi Ischmael*, Vienna, 1865.

Weiss, I. H., *Sifra*, Vienna, 1862.

Weiss, I. H., *Zur Geschichte der jüdischen Tradition*, (*Theil 3*), Vienna, 1871—1891.

Wünsche, A., *Die Vorstellungen vom Zustande nach dem Tode nach Apokryphen, Talmud und Kirchenvätern*, *JPTh.*, vol. VI, 1880, pp. 355—313, 195—523.

APHRAATES AND THE JEWS

By FRANK GAVIN, General Theological Seminary, New York

I. OF THE GENERAL CHARACTER OF THE HOMILIES.

The "Persian Sage", ܚܟܝܡܐ ܦܪܣܝܐ, now known to be Aphraates, wrote in the years 336—345 A. D. twenty-three homilies in Syriac, which have been carefully edited and are available for use in two editions.[1] Their peculiar interest lies not only in the fact that they are almost unique in the purity of their diction and are in fact the standard texts of classical Syriac,[2] but, as well, in the intrinsic interest of their thought. Aphraates is the sole surviving representative of a type of Christian thought which was essentially Semitic, and utterly independent of both Latin and Greek philosophy. The medium of his thinking, classical Syriac, was far closer to the contemporary Jewish Aramaic of Babylon, than was the Syriac of the later Christian writers. Even in St. Ephraim Syrus[3] can be discerned a transition type toward the later Syriac, bristling with Greek and Latin philosophical and theological terms, with

---

[1] Bibliography, Nos. 1 and 2. For discussion of his name, life, works, chronology, etc., cf. introduction to Parisot's work, pp. ix—xl; Forget, *De vita et scriptis Aphraatis*, pp. 1—223; A. Bert, *Aphraat's des persischen Weisen Homilien*, ... pp. vii—xxxvi; Saase's, *Prolegomena*, etc.

[2] Nöldeke in *Gött. Gelehrt. Auss.*, 1869, pp. 1521—32, and *Mandäische Grammatik*, p. xx.

[3] On him and a comparison of his theology with that of Aph. cf. F. C. Burkitt *Early Eastern Christianity*, New York, 1904, especially pp. 103—110, etc.

its syntax broken down and its character completely debased by
an enforced conformance to an only half understood Greek idiom.
This subservience of thought and servility of style issued in a
double calamity. (a) In the centuries in which Syriac literature
flourished there emerges almost no thinker or writer half so pro-
lific in thought as in literary output. (b) In these centuries the
artificiality and imitative character of Syriac writers destroyed
the structure of their medium. Under them Syriac was twisted
into false and unnatural shapes in imitation of an alien Greek
thought and idiom. As Renan observes in „*De Philosophia Peri-
patetica apud Syros,*" (1852, p. 3)[1] „the characteristic of the Syrians
is a certain mediocrity." In Aphraates, however, the classical
language is at its best, and his homilies are worthy of philological
study as fine examples of the linguistic excellence of pure and
idiomatic Syriac.[2]

The language of Aph. is free from any borrowing of technical
philosophical terms. Any peculiarly alien properties of borrowed
words had been strained off by successive filtrations, or assimilated
and their identily lost in the mass of the language as a whole.
The process whereby such words as ܠܐܝ or ܐܘܣܝܐ[3] had been
added to the vocabulary of Syriac had antedated Aphraates. It
is only by reference to subsequent theological development that
a fixed theological or philosophical content can be read into these
words in the *Homilies.* There is no philosophical system discernible in any part of the whole text. Later Syriac writers worked

---

[1] Quoted by Wright, *Syriac Literature*, pp. 1—2.

[2] Any good Syriac grammar draws heavily on the homilies, — *e. g.*, Nöldeke's
and Duval's. For an intensive study of Aph.'s syntax, of which only the treatment
of the relative is available, cf. E. Hartwig, *Untersuchungen zur Syntax des Afraates..*,
Leipzig. 1893.

[3] E. g., ܩܢܘܡܐ : 161 : 16; 284 : 19; 285 : 10; 332 : 4; 11 : 21 : 12; 11 : 125 : 7;
11 : 144 : 8, in each case means simply "self", though it may be from ἐπικείμενον,
and have had originally a definite philosophical content. Cf. ܩܢܘܡ and the word
itself in later uses, in Payne Smith *Thesaurus.* Thus too, ܟܝܢܐ : 36 : 14; 156 : 2;
225 : 22 — 23; 261 : 1; 277 . 21 — 23, etc., never has a technical meaning,
and = only "nature" or "character." So also with ܠܐܝ or ܐܘܣܝܐ : 100 : 18 — 19;
11 : 117 : 11 = οὐσία, but in no technical or philosophical sense. Cf. Bethune-Baker
Nestorius and his Teaching, appendix, pp. 212 — 232, (ed. of 1908) on the Syriac
use of this term.

from the basis of a philosophy with which they harmonized the Sacred Literature, in much the same way as Philo adjusted his interpretation of the Torah to his philosophy. Earlier Greek and Latin writers had pursued this method — particularly is this the case with the Apologists. The apologetic of Aphraates was not at all of this character.

While the case for Christianity must of necessity have been put into the terms in which any given controversy was conducted, it is perhaps unique in Christian literature that in his apologetic Aphraates did not seek to accommodate his belief to an alien medium. As he worked from his theology outward to as near an approach as he ever made to a philosophy, (and not as did most of his contemporaries, who reversed the process,) so in his apologetic there is practically no difference in method from that which might as fitly be called a dogmatic. Christian literature may be divided into the two general types, on the basis of the relation between theology and philosophy. If philosophy be the starting point, and the object of the writer be to harmonize, adjust, and interpret theological belief in relation to it, it is obvious that the content of what is held to be revealed truth, that is, dogma, would sustain vastly different treatment than if the process of thinking and presentation were conditioned by the aim of presenting and expounding the received content of belief independently of the dominant philosophical necessity. Presenting the case of Christianity, defending it from attack, explaining, and interpreting it, in short, the task of the apologete, has usually been held to involve a certain translation of traditional belief into current philosophical language. A body of doctrine may remain the same and its defence and method of propagation differ in different periods, as the accent of interest and point of contact or attack shift. It is, however, of singular interest that no *a priori* philosophy determines the thought of Aphraates. No current idiom of philosophy conditions the presentation of his thought.

Of the twenty-three *Homilies*, the first ten were written in the years 336—337.[1] They were written upon the request of a friend,

[1] cf. Hom. V, paragraph 5, particularly, 193 : 17 — 25; Hom. X, paragraph 9, and 1044 : 10 — 15.

also a monk, and probably the head of another community of monks. He had asked for an "explanation concerning matters necessary to the faith" that by such an exposition his mind might be "set at rest" (ﺍﺳﺘﺮﺍﺡ).[1] It is possible that this is a literary fiction. The form is very reminiscent of the "dedication" of St. Luke's Gospel and the opening words of the Acts.[2] In any case, the first ten homilies were written for a larger audience than one person, for they were to be read and discussed with his brother monks.[3] There is in them no explicit dogmatic teaching, and no attempt made, as Dom Connolly has pointed out,[4] to give an ordered exposition of the content and meaning of the Christian Faith. It is the "works of the Faith" which he is to discuss, that is, the implications of it in their practical bearing; for example, the titles of some of these homilies are, "On Faith" (Hom. I), "On Love" (Hom II), "On Fasting" (III), "On Prayer" (IV), "Concerning Monks" (VI), "On Penitents" (VII), "On Humility" (IX). That Aphraates writes as he does in *Homilies* VI, VII, and X, shows at once his own authority and, one may justly infer, the condition and circumstances of those for whom he wrote. They were monks, and his friend was probably the head of a monastery. (cf. Hom. X "On Pastors".) Laxity[5] and the domestic problems of the monastery are reflected in the conditions presupposed in homilies VI ("On monks") and VII ("On Penitents").

Of more interest to the study I am about to present is the homily „On Wars" (V) which contains scarcely veiled references

---

[1] 4:20—22.

[2] St Luke 1:1—4; Acts 1:1.

[3] 465:1—6.

[4] Dom R H. Connolly, O. S. B. *The Creed of Aphraates*, in ZNTW, Vol. 7 (1906), pp. 204, ff. and cf. the controversy with Burkitt,—F. C. Burkitt, *Early Eastern Christianity*, pp. 81—95; 120—141; Connolly in *J. Th. S.*, Vol. 6, (1904—5), Vol. 6, pp. 522—539; Burkitt, *ibid*, pp. 286—290; Connolly, *ibid.* in Vol. 8, pp. 10—15; *ibid.*, pp. 41—48, etc.

[5] cf. 456:23—25, and on Aph.'s own status, cf. Hom. XIV, which is practically an encyclical letter written by a prelate to a council, on the date and circumstances concerning which homily cf. Parisot's introduction, pp. xviii—xxi, Forget, *op. cit.*, pp 200—204; Antonelli, in Gallandius, *Bibliotheca veterum Patrum*, Vol. V, pp. 3 ff. (Ed. of 1756, Rome); G. Ryssel, *Brief des Georgs*, introduction, etc. Kmosko, in *Patr. Syr., pars prima*, t. II, pp. 701, ff.

to the war between Persia and Rome. The progress of this war caused much anxiety and distress to the Christian communities.[1] It was for the reason that he wished to hearten them, discuss the situation, and make a prophecy of a happy outcome of the then untoward circumstances that led him to disguise it all "in figures" (ܦܠܐܬܐ). He uses the prophecy as a veil beneath which lies his real meaning. Its significance will be hidden from the possibly hostile glance of a casual reader and apparent to one who has the key to the secret. Rome is the great power. It is the iron legs and feet of the image of Dan. 2[39-41].[2] After quoting Ezek. 15[4-5], he goes on to say that the vine of Is. 5[3-6] is Christ, and that "He at His coming gave (the power to) rule to the Romans, called the 'sons of Esau,' who hold the rule for Him who had committed it to them."[3] It is owing to the obstinate pride of Persia that its fall is assured.[4] The armies of Rome will not be defeated by the forces gathered together against them, for they will hold the kingdom for Him who had committed it to their trust, who Himself is its Keeper and Preserver.[5] The cause of Rome is the cause of Jesus, and it will not fail to conquer.[6] This is the essence of the homily, though the conclusion[7] is in a homiletic and devotional strain.

This homily throws some light on the conditions in the Christian communities of Persia which led to the persecution. The Persian Empire was "the beast about to be slain".[8] Although he disclaims any special revelation, yet Aphraates means his words to be taken as a prophecy. He bases his prediction on the text of St. Luke 14[11] and the analogy of God's method of dealing with mankind in the past.[9] This is not the first prophecy which has been proven false in the event. From other sources we are enabled to

---

[1] 184:1—4; 185:3—5.
[2] 208:25—27; 212:19:23, cf. Parisot's introduction, sec. 12 and 20.
[3] 229:26—27; 232:1—2.
[4] cf. homily V, sec. 3, 5, 7, etc.
[5] 233:12—15.
[6] 233:16—21.
[7] sec. 25.
[8] 237:18.
[9] 237:10—20.

reconstruct much of the background of his times. The preference
for Rome and Roman rule was not due solely to the profession of Christianity by its rulers. In the Persian Empire the
Christians were regarded as a slave class, treated constantly without consideration, and subject without the recourse of appeal to
the whims and fancies of merciless overlords. Furthermore, there
was the glamor of ancient Rome and the strength and power of
its organization. Above all, however, the outstanding fact was
that this empire was now under a king of their own faith. If the
letter of Constantine to Sapur[1] of about the year 330 be authentic,
it shows an extensive familiarity with conditions in the Persian
Empire. It is written in the tone of one who feels himself con-
stituted the Protector and Advocate of all Christians in all places.
Sapur began to reign in the year 309 on September fifth,[2] and
in the year 337—338 attacked Nisibis, the first act of his successful
war against Rome.[3] To maintain the war Sapur had to exact
heavier taxes and to conscript troops. It was in the course of
the campaign that the persecutions of the Christians became violent.
While there had been before this time occasional acts of persecution, the great necessity to which the Persian Empire was put
made an undoubted loyalty to the royal policy imperative.

This support the Christians had not formerly given; note the
rebellion in Adiabene, through which Mar Kardagh at death attained
a martyr's fame.[4] In the year 318 had occurred the martyrdoms
of three Christians in Karka de Beit S'lokh,[5] and in 327 there are

---

[1] *De vita Constantini*, Eusebius, IV : 9 — 14, in *Die griechische christliche Schrift-
steller*, Leipzig, 1902, Eusebius, I. Band, pp. 121, ff.

[2] *Tabari*, ed. Th. Nöldeke, p. 411.

[3] Though Nisibis did not fall till 363, when it was ceded to the Romans after
the defeat of Julian the Apostate. It had been by the treaty of Narses and Galerian
surrendered to the Romans in 297. St. James of Nisibis succeeded in driving off
Sapur in his three unsuccessful attempts upon the city.

[4] *Die Geschichte des Mar Abdisho und seines Jüngers Mar Kardagh*, Ed. Feige,
Keil, 1889; *Acta Mar Cadaghi Assyriae praefecti*, J. Abbeloos, Brussells, 1890; *Acta
Martyrum et Sanctorum*, P. Bedjan, Leipzig, 1890—97, t. II, pp. 442—506; R. Duval,
La littérature Syriaque, pp. 137, ff.

[5] Georg Hoffmann, *Auszüge aus syrischen Akten persischer Märtyrer*, Leipzig, 1886,
pp. 9, ff.; Bedjan, t. II, pp. 1—56.

recorded eleven martyrdoms in the province of Arzanene.[1] When Sapur sent out instructions ordering the drafting of recruits and collection of taxes to prosecute the war against Rome, (which had begun so inauspiciously in his repulse at Nisibis in 337—338) he was met by reluctance, passivity, and even opposition, on the part of the Christians.

For the facts concerning this period we have the *Passion* of St. Simeon bar Sabba'e, the *Homilies* of Aphraates, Tabari, and Byzantine hagiographic material as authorities. The fifth homily of Aph. gave a forecast of the storm impending.

The second series of Aphraates' *Hom lies* give us more definite and important information as to the events which occurred after the outbreak of the war with Rome. As we have seen, the state of mind reflected in homily V is one of as open and frank hostility to Persia as of outspoken advocacy of the cause of Rome. It had become a religious war in the minds of those who came within range of Aphraates' teaching. In the fourteenth, twenty-first, and twenty-second homilies he gives us other indications of the progress of events. In homily fourteen the calamities of which he writes later could not have occurred, for therein he complains of the ambition and worldliness of the clergy, which, as Kmosko notes, is a characteristic of times of peace, not of persecution.[2] It is dated the thirty-fifth year of Sapur, that is, 344[3]. This encyclical was inserted into the second group of homilies, the "controversial homilies",[4] which are dated 343—45[5]. The twenty-third homily ("On the Cluster", — cf. Isaiah 65[8], 2 Esd. 9[21]) while it is primarily a theodicy and not an apologetic, yet this

---

[1] At his time under Roman rule, hence their death was not during an organized Persian persecution, but probably in a raid by hostile anti-Christian Persians. cf. *Acta Sanctorum Martyrum*, ed. Steph. Evodius Assemani, Rome, 1748, *pars* I, pp. 215—224. cf. J. Labourt *Le christianisme dans l'empire perse*, pp. 50 (note), and 78.

[2] cf. *S. Simeon bar Sabba'e*, ed. M. Kmosko, in *Pat. Syr. pars prima*, T. II, pp. 699—701; Aphraates, 577: 1—5: 625: 16—18. Still a dark cloud was hanging over the Church, as can be inferred from the whole tone of the encyclical, (cf. 573: 15—19; 709: 12—16,) though the church's chief difficulties were internal friction, pride, and worldliness.

[3] 725: 1—2.

[4] *i. e.*, nos. XI—XIII, XV—XXI.

[5] 1044: 15—20.

characteristic, though incidental, is sufficient to constitute its claim
to be included in the "controversial" group. It is designed to
stabilize and hearten the Christians who were now in the midst
of persecution. Aphraates speaks of a "persecution which came
in the fifth year after the destruction of the churches, in the year
of the great slaughter of confessors in the Eastern country."[1] It
is dated in the next year after the twenty-second homily —
(namely, 345), which closes this (second) series.

In the year 344 occurred the martyrdom of St. Simeon bar
Sabba'e, of whom we have an authentic *Passion*, and another later
work concerning him.[2] Kmosko dates the first recension (MS[1])
in the year 474, and says that it contains an account written
before 407. The second recension (MS[2]) was written toward the
end of the fifth century. The first he finds to bear good evidences,
internal and external, of authenticity,[3] and reference to it confirms
the inference already drawn as to the cause of the persecution
and to the condition of the Christians reflected in the Homilies.

In the royal command purporting to have been issued for the
arrest of St. Simeon (given in the second recension of his martyrdom),
there is the following statement: "Wars and tribulations which
are grievous to us and the gods, to them (the Christians) are life
and delights, for while they live in our land, they cleave in mind
to Caesar our enemy."[4] Thus, too, the Jews tell Sapur (according
to the first recension) that were he to send gifts and presents to
the Roman Emperor they would be spurned, but if Simeon were
to write him but a mean letter it would be received with reverence,
and his wishes immediately carried out.[5] When St. Simeon came
as prisoner, he refused to reverence the King, which before, as

[1] II:149:1—11. On the dates cf. Parisot, pp. XV—XVII. It may be that
Aph. himself fell in the persecution of Christians which lasted throughout Sapur's
reign, i e. till 379. W. Wright in *An Ancient Syriac Martyrology*, *J. S. L.*,
Vol. VIII (old series — 1866) p. 431, gives the name of a martyr Aphraates. The
text is authentic, and is of 412 or earlier.

[2] Ed. by M. Kmosko, with Latin translation and excellent introductions. On the
chronology of the persecution cf. pp. 690—713.

[3] cf. discussion. *op. cit.*, 678—690.

[4] St. Sim. b. Sabba'e, *op. cit.*, 791:12—16.

[5] *ibid.*, 739:4—12.

a free man, he had not refused to do.[1] In both recensions the purpose is patent: the writer wishes to show that the persecution was directly due to the hatred of Sapur for Christianity. Just so far is this true as the national cause of Persia was identified with the forces against Christian Rome. As we have seen, if to Aphraates the cause of Rome were the cause of Jesus, it is not unlikely that the Persians recognized that the cause of Persia was the cause of the forces against Christianity. In this sense the contention of the two *martyrdoms* that it was a religious persecution, is true.

From other sources we are confirmed in this view of the conditions. A large Christian community existed in the midst of a non-Christian state, which, while it was in peace, did not greatly disturb itself over religious matters. In times of danger, however, profession of Christianity was tantamount to treason and disloyalty, and the persecution viewed politically as a part of the struggle of Persia against Rome, might be regarded religiously as a persecution directed against Christianity. Persecution was usually sporadic, and localized in towns and centres of government or religious control.[2] A Christian was accused and denounced, then arrested, imprisoned, "questioned," and upon failure to recant, executed.[3]

It would seem at first sight rather unexpected that of the homilies written during this period the bulk should deal with anti-Jewish controversy. But in both recensions of the passion of St. Simeon, the redactor shows great anti-Jewish feeling. It was the Jews who calumniated St. Simeon before Sapur, and made the very telling point noted above, concerning the status of the Bishop Simeon in the eyes of the Roman Emperor.[4] Simeon prophesies another slaughter of the Jews, of which an account is given in the second

---

[1] *ibid.*, 742:11—26.

[2] Labourt, *Le Christianisme dans l'empire perse*, pp. 56—63.

[3] The internal evidence of the *acta martyrum*, collected by Bedjan and others, is born out by other documents in non-Semitic sources, *e. g.*, Sozomen in the second book of his *Historia Ecclesiastica*. Much of the evidence is in *Memoires pour servir à l'Histoire ecclésiastique*, by Tillemont, t. VII, pp. 76—101; 236—242. Cf. *S. Sadoth Episcopi Seleuciae et Ctesiphontis Acta Graeca.* H. Delahaye, S. J., (in *Analecta Bollandiana, T. XXI. fasc. II*).

[4] cf. *S. Sim. b. Sab., op. cit.*, Sec. 13. This is embodied also in the second recension — cf. 807:5—14, *ibid.*

recension.[1] This account is to the effect that during the time of
Julian, who had proclaimed to the Jews his readiness to assist
and further the rebuilding of the Temple in Jerusalem,[2] a number
of Jews left Machuza "in the hope of this return and had gone
three parasangs' distance from the city. When news of this was
brought to Sapur he sent his troops and slew many thousands of
them . . . ."[3] If the account of his massacre be authentic, the Jews
suffered a persecution of much the same quality as the Christians,
and for the same reasons.

According to Labourt, the Jews were thought to have informed
upon St. Simeon's sister, Tarbo, and her sister-nuns.[4] Just how
much truth there is in the assertion that the Jews urged Sapur
on in persecuting the Christians, it is difficult to determine. Nöldeke
thinks it very likely,[5] but Duval is by no means convinced on the
basis of the evidence of the *Acta*.[6] The relation between Jews
and Christians in Mesopotamia was always delicate, and the situation
that lay back of the controversial homilies, was one which, under
the stress of persecution, made the Christian less sparing than ever
of recrimination. The causes of the friction were many. Before
proceeding to a study of the evidence offered as to the relation
of Christians and Jews by the *Homilies*, it will be well to consider
first, the history of Persian Christianity, with especial reference to
its probable relation to Judaism, and, second, to investigate the
position of the Jews under the Sassanids.

---

1 Sections 14, 15.

2 For the decree, cf. H. Graetz, *Geschichte der Juden*, Leipzig, 1888, Vol. II,
pp. 179—183.

3 *Patrol. Syr.*, *pars prima*, t. II, 811:4—6. There seems to be no record of
this event in Jewish literature, so far as I have been able to discover. Cf. M. Adler,
J. Q. R., Vol. 5, 1899, "*The Emperor Julian and the Jews.*"

4 J. Labourt, *Le christianisme dans l'empire Perse*, p. 58. He refers to Assemani,
Acta Martyrum (Orientalium), *ed. cit.*, pp. 54 and 69, and *Hist. Eccl.* of Sozomen,
II, 12, in Migne's *Patrol. Graeca*, LXVII, col. 955; *Acta Martyr.*, Bedjan, Vol. II,
pp. 254—260.

5 *Geschichte der Perser und Araber zur Zeit der Sassaniden*, (of Tabari), ed.
Theodore Nöldeke, p. 68, note i.

6 *La littérature Syriaque*, R. Duval, p. 134.

II. Of the Origin and Constituency of the Church of Aphraates.

It is not until the Persian Church, by a process of reflection and under the stimulus of a kind of national self-consciousness, began to construct for itself a past as honorable as her position in the 5th century warranted, that any well defined and carefully articulated written tradition appears. Three main traditions are recorded. The first is that of Timothy I, a Nestorian patriarch, who in a letter to the Maronite monks says that the Magi on their return brought the Gospel to Persia "five years before Nestorius, and twenty after the Ascension of our Lord."[1] The gap of some four centuries in the legend disposes of any value in it as history. The second legend makes the Apostle St. Thomas the founder of the see of Seleucia-Ctesiphon, and the earliest list of bishops is in the works of Elias of Damascus (*circ.* 890).[2] Together with various lists of former occupants of the see, a letter of the "Fathers of the West" (that is, the Bishops subject to Antioch) guarantees the autonomy of the see of Seleucia, certifies its patriarchal character, and assumes its independence of Antioch.[3] The value of this is easily tested by noticing that the reputed bearer of the "letter" was Agapetus, bishop of Beit Lapat, who was one of the orators at the synod of Dadisho held in 424.[4] The third legend binds up the history of the origin of Persian Christianity with Edessa. Addai, according to this third tradition, evangelized the valley of the Tigris.[5] Thus, too, say the *Acta Maris*.[6] This legend is shown by Duval[7] to be useless historically, since the document is of the sixth century or later. The work was composed merely to advance the reputation of an obscure town, Dar Qoni.[8]

---

[1] From an unedited MS., (Borgia, K. VI, 4, p. 653,) quoted by Labourt, *op. cit.*, p. 10.

[2] *ibid.*, p. 11, quoting *Bibl. Orient.*, t. *II*, p. 392.

[3] Barhebraeus, *Chronicum Ecclesiast.*, II, p. 26, *Ed.* Abbeloos-Lamy, Louvain, 1874.

[4] *Synodicon orientale*, *Ed.* J. Chabot, in *Notices et Extraits des Manuscrits*, t. XXXVII. (*Récueil des actes synodaux de l'Église de Perse*) p. 294.

[5] *Synodicon orientale*, Chabot, p. 581.

[6] *Ed.* Abbeloos, Louvain, 1885.

[7] *La littérature Syriaque*, p. 118.

[8] cf. Labourt, *op. cit.*, pp. 14—15.

After a careful examination of the evidence regarding the origins of Christianity in Edessa, it would seem highly probable that it was due to the missionary activity of Palestinian Jewish Christians. According to Burkitt, the original Judeo-Christian character of the Edessene Church was later reinforced and substantially altered to align it with the general western type of the Great Church.[1] The glory of Rome (where Serapion of Antioch was consecrated early in the third century), influenced even the obscure community of Christians in the eastern outpost of Edessa, who could thus boast of communion with the see of Peter. But the overlay of the more developed type of Christianity never succeeded in effacing entirely the original character of primitive Edessene Christianity. Edessene Christianity was due originally to missionary enterprise, and sustained its character in the years to come. The case made by Burkitt is strengthened, if the various indications of alliance between Edessa and Mesopotamian Christianity of the early type be kept in mind. It would seem probable that the Church of northern Mesopotamia, which reproduces the same characteristics as are indicated in the early type of Edessene Christianity, owed its evangelization to the activity of missionaries from Edessa.

From Edessa a great road led across to Mardin, Nisibis, and thence to Mosul[2] It would have been the obvious route by which the early Edessene converts, on fire with the Christian evangel, would propagate their faith, and convey to others what had been brought them through like missionary activity. Such intercourse would have been difficult, if not impossible, after the rise of the Sassanids. The tradition above referred to from the *Acta Maris* may really embody a germ of truth when it claims the apostle of Edessa as the founder of Persian Christianity, if the obvious course of missionary activity had been from Edessa eastward and then perhaps towards the south. Armenian Christianity traces its

[1] The whole argument may be found in *Early Eastern Christianity*, by F. C. Burkitt, London, 1904, pp. 1—79, particularly, pp. 34, 76; Tixeront, *Les origines de l'Eglise d'Edesse*, Paris, 1888; R. Duval, *L'histoire d'Edesse*, Paris, 1892.

[2] s. v. "Mesopotamia," by Albrecht Socin, in *Encycl. Britt.*, Vol. XVI, Ninth ed., (American issue), Chicago, 1892, p. 53, and cf. bibliography, p. 56; according to Socin, the early Persian roads were as excellent as those of Rome; cf. on this also Graetz, *op.* and *vol. cit.*

origin to Edessa,[1] and, according to Sozomen, shared with Edessa in evangelizing Persia.[2] Armenia, as Labourt points out,[3] was too new in the faith thus early to establish missions abroad, even if its foundation had been laid by the time of the first decades of the third century.[4] Yet Edessa from the beginning of this century was a centre of great missionary activity.[5] The alliance, — probably via Edessa — with Antioch is suggested in the History of Beit S'lokh,[6] in which a Greek is recorded as the first bishop of that city.

If Burkitt's contention that the original Christian community of Edessa was composed of Jewish converts be true; and if northern Mesopotamia was evangelized from Edessa before the primitive character of its Christianity had been made to align itself with contemporaneous Greek or Roman Christianity, we should expect to find strong Jewish affinities of thought, expression, and general viewpoint, in the Semitic Christianity of Northern Mesopotamia. If Aphraates represent a type of Christian thought which disappeared even from Edessa within a few years after the close of the second century[7], we should expect to find traces in him of both a primitive and undeveloped theology, containing strong Jewish elements and, as well, traces of the thought current in the second century. As a matter of fact, we do find a strong alliance in his general Christology with that of the so-called "Asianic" school, particularly with St. Irenaeus of Lyons.[8] We

[1] E. Ter Minassiantz, *Die armenische Kirche in ihrer Beziehung zu der syrischen Kirche*, 1904, T. u. U.

[2] *Historia ecclesiastica*, II, 8, in Migne, *Patr. Graec.*, t. LXVII, col. 956.

[3] *op. cit.*, p. 18.

[4] cf. Ter Minassiantz, *op. cit.*

[5] R. Duval, *Les Origines de l'Église d'Édesse*, Paris, 1888; *Histoire d'Édesse*, 1880; Lipsius, *Die Edessenische Abgarsage*; A. Harnack, *Die Mission und Ausbreitung des Christentums in den ersten drei Jahrhunderten*, 1903, pp. 440 ff. (giving patristic evidence on early Mesopotamian Christianity).

[6] G. Hoffmann, *Auszüge aus syrischen Akten persischer Märtyrer*, Leipzig, 1886, p. 46.

[7] On the relation of Aph.' thought to the primitive stratum of Edessene Christianity, *i. e.*, that of the original Judeo-Christians, cf. F. C. Burkitt, *Early Christianity outside the Roman Empire*, p. 61, where he compares Bardesanes and Aph., illustrating this relationship.

[8] cf. Excursus VI in my dissertation, *The Christology of Aphraates*. His Christology had not developed beyond the type of St. Irenaeus.

find also interesting affiliations, first suggested by G. Bert,[1] with the type represented in the *Didache*. This I shall hope to discuss below, after I have treated of the *Homilies*.

There are not a few indications that the Christians of northern Mesopotamia were Jewish converts .. The version of the O. T. which they used was the *Peshitta*. This version, as Nestlé notes,[2] follows both the Hebrew text and Jewish exegesis. While Isaiah and the Twelve Minor Prophets contain much from the LXX, Ezekiel and Proverbs are much more like the Targumim.[3] The book of Chronicles has midrashic affiliations.[4] It has been conjectured that the Peshitta translation, almost certainly done by Jews — since there are many cross relations to the Targumim, — the "Pasuka," Psalm 68[18], chapter superscriptions, the translation of "Selah," according to the Targumic code — was used in the synagogue worship in Palestine, and was completely supplanted later on by the Targumim. The evidence for this, with Talmudic references, would seem to furnish a very high degree of probability for the thesis.[5] Yet the question of its authorship is still unsettled. "The origin of the Peshitta is still as obscure as when Theodore of Mopsuestia wrote: ἡρμήνευται δὲ ταῦτα εἰς μὲν τὴν τῶν Σύρων παρ' ὅτου δήποτε, οὐδὲ γὰρ ἔγνωσται μέχρι τῆς τήμερον ὅστις ποτὲ οὗτός ἐστιν."[6]

Of great interest is the fact that the terms for "salvation," the verb "to save," the noun "Saviour," for which the O. T. Peshitta uses the equivalents ܦܘܪܩܢܐ, ܦܪܩ; and ܦܪܘܩܐ, — are in the early Syriac Gospels translated ܐܚܝ for σώζειν, and ܚܝܐ for σωτήριον.[7] Aphraates,

---

[1] *op. cit.*, p. 18, note 2; p. 19, note 1.

[2] Nestlé, *Text und Übersetzungen der Bibel*, Leipzig. 1897, pp. 230—231.

[3] On the Peshitto, cf. Wright, *History of Syriac Literature*, pp. 3—6; R. Duval, *La littérature syriaque*, pp. 31—43, s. v. "Peshitto" in *J. E.*, Vol. IX, pp. 653—655.

[4] cf. II Kings 23:9 נכה פרעה = ܣܝܒܪ ܡܚܐ, ܦܘܪܩ, and II Chron. 35:20-24. The midrashic explanation of this = נכה רגלים. Aph. quotes the text, 972:6—7, and 11:60:16, on which cf. Parisot, *op. cit.*, praef. sec. 12, p. xli, and note 1. cf. also I Chron. 5:2. ܡܝ, ܘܗܝ ܐ̈ܘܗ̇ ܩܦܡ ܠܕܗܡ ܠܟܠܡ ܡܚܐܡܚ = יהודה נבר .... ולנגיד ממנו.

[5] It is conveniently summarized in the article in the *J. E.*, *cit. sup.*, vol. IX, pp. 635—5; *e. g.*, cf. Ex. 22:30, Ḥul. 102b and Targum *ad. loc.*; Lev. 167 and Ḥul. 11a; Lev. 18:21 and Meg. 25a; Lev. 24:8 and Men. 97a, etc.

[6] H. B. Swete, *Introduction to the Old Testament in Greek*, Cambridge, 1902, p. 112.

[7] cf. Payne-Smith, *Thesaurus*, col. 3293. for O. T. references, and those in the later Syriac N. T. versions.

who used the Diatessaron with its early form of text,[1] always makes "to live," = "to be saved."[2] Thus, "only believe and thy daughter shall be saved," where σωθήσεται of St. Lk. 8⁵⁰ = ܠܘܠ.[3] "Salvation is identified in the Syriac usage with 'life'. Σωτήρ is ܡܚܝܢܐ, "Life-Giver," and 'to be saved' is 'to live . . .' This is the more remarkable as Syriac has several words meaning 'to deliver,' 'to protect,' 'to be safe and sound.' May we not therefore believe that this identification of 'salvation' and 'life' is the genuine Aramaic usage, and that the Greek Gospels have in this instance introduced a distinction which was not made by Christ and His Aramaic-speaking disciples?"[4] Subsequent Syriac versions aligned the older version used in the Diatessaron to the standard of theological thought and feeling of a later date, but in Aphraates as a typical, and perhaps unique, example of early northern Mesopotamian Christianity, no such alterations appear as were made later in the N. T. "Peshitta" of the fifth century.[5]

It has been conjectured that this original O. S. version was the work of Jewish Christians, by whose efforts it was given to the Gentiles whom they in turn evangelized.[6] It would seem highly likely that the community of Christians in northern Mesopotamia, to whom the Edessene converts brought Christianity, were themselves Jews, — at least in the earliest years of that mission. The earliest name for "Christian" in northern Mesopotamia was "Nazarenes" (ܢܨܪ̈ܝܐ). This is the common title at even so late a period as that

---

[1] On the early Syriac versions and the Diatessaron, cf. *Die altsyrische Evangelien-übersetzung und Tatians Diatessaron*, A. Hjelt, Leipzig, 1903; *Forschungen zur Geschichte des N. T. — Kanons u. d. altk. Lit.*, Th. Zahn, vii Theil, Heft 1.

[2] St. Mk. 16¹⁶ — Aph. 41 : 3 — 4.

[3] Aph. 40 : 21 — 22.

[4] *Early Christianity outside the Roman Empire*, F. C. Burkitt, p. 22; Gerhardt Vos, in *H. B. D.*, vol. 11, pp. 553—557; *Über σώζειν und seine Derivata im N. T.*, W. Wagner in *Z. N. T W.*, 1905, (vol. 6, Heft 3) pp. 205—225. On the Syriac use of ܡܚܝ, cf. Payne-Smith, *Thes.*, col. 1252 of vol. I.

[5] cf. Burkitt, *op. cit.*, pp. 88—99, on the "Holy Spirit" in Aphraates. The conclusions he draws from these facts I believe unjustified in their entirety, but he draws attention to the undoubted character of the evidence. The N. T. "Peshitto" is dated cir. 412.

[6] *Praefatio, caput* I, to his edition of St. Simeon bar Sabba'e in *Patrol. Syr.*, pars I, tomus 2, no. 2, pp. 662—664.

of the *Acta Martyrum*.[1] The Jews at the indictment of St. Simeon bar Sabba'e used the word as the common designation of Christians, by which time (*circ. V saec.*) it must long have lost its original meaning of Judeo-Christian.[2] It is a characteristically Jewish usage that שם or שמא = אלהים. The Christian adoption of this use may be found in the earlier recension of the Martyrdom of St. Simeon, (MS, — 4th cent.)[3] Thus a martyred bishop of the name of ܠܐܙܪ of the town Ḥnaitha has the same name as ܠܐܙܪ of Karka-d'Beit-S'lokh.[4] Kmosko gives examples of other conspicuously Jewish uses and ideas adopted by Christians, recorded in the *Acta* of the Persian martyrs, such as the reckoning of time, the prostration towards the East, chiliasm, etc.[5] It is hardly possible that such considerable common elements and Christian-Jewish affiliations should have been the result merely of "friendly intercourse" of the Christians with the Jews,[6] between whom at this time, because of the lack of evidence in Talmud and Midrash, Funk finds no reason to suspect any hostility or unfriendliness.[7] The evidence from both *Acta* and the *Homil es* interprets this silence in Jewish sources for us. The Christian communities, especially in the north, were in such a numerical minority that in normal times it was essential to keep on good terms with their Jewish neighbors. The organization of the Christian communities[8] near Mosul, for example, was such that in towns the Christian lay folk were few in number

---

1 Thus: "in the thirtieth year of Sapur . . . there came Magi slandering the ܡܪܝܐ," *Acta Martyrum*, Bedjan, t. ii, Leipzig, 1891, p. 55. For a criticism, summary, and analysis of these *acta*, cf. Labourt, *op. cit.*, pp. 51—82.

2 cf. *Patrol. Syr.*, *pars prima*, *t. 2*, in S. Sim. b. Sab., 791: 7—10; 799: 14; 818: 13; 867: 23.

3 *ibid.*, 747: 22.

4 Given by Kmosko, *op. cit.*, p. 663, and cf. note 3.

5 *ibid.*

6 *Die haggadischen Elemente in den Homilien des Aphraates*, Sol. Funk, Vienna, 1891, pp. 10—12.

7 s. v. "Aphraates," L. Ginzberg, in *J. E.*, *loc. cit*, notes the absence of bitterness in his reference to Jews in the earlier homilies of Aphraates.

8 On which cf. *Untersuchungen über den persischen Weisen*, P. Schwen, Berlin, 1907, pp. 18—38; *Le christianisme dans l'empire perse*, Labourt, pp. 28—42; the Burkitt-Connolly controversy, in J. T. S., vol 6 (1904—5), pp. 522—539; (cf. *Early Eastern Christianity*, F. C. Burkitt, 125—141); J. T. S., ibid, pp. 286—290; J. T. S., vol. 8 (1906—7), pp. 41—48, and cf. bibliography.

and not particularly powerful, either socially or intellectually. Even the well established communities of monks were in danger from the cogency of the reasoning of the Jews; and one can read between the lines in Aphraates, — particularly in the later homilies — a solicitude and anxiety not unmixed with fear. It is obvious that the Jews had nothing to fear from the Christians. It is abundantly clear that the Christians feared the Jews.

Both the attitude of the Jews, as reflected in the *Acta* and *Homilies*, and also the curious cross-relations in thought and expression in these sources can be accounted for, if it were true that the early Christians in northern Mesopotamia had been converts from Judaism. Aphraates himself was a gentile convert, but his type of theology, the methods and content of his exegesis, the general characteristics of even his Christology, are all typical of a stage of development which had no representative in his day, either in the place of its origin, Edessa, or even in other parts of his own country. His theology is widely different in thought from that of the *Narratio* of St. Simeon bar Sabba'e. The simple Christology, the absence of Nicene terminology, the total lack of any considerable theological reflection, all point to a primitive type, beyond which the thought of, for example, the great southern see of Seleucia-Ctesiphon had developed to some considerable degree. The *Homilies* represent a much simpler theology, while the Christian community to the south is of a type more in line with the thinking and reflection of Catholic Christendom. While the north was chiefly Semitic in its general term of thought and expression, Seleucia was more nearly in these respects like Hellenic Christendom. The Acta S. Maris record that before St. Maris' coming there had been no Christians at Seleucia.[1] Seleucia was a city of Greeks, too, and this may well account for the non-Semitic cast of its theology as shown in the *Acta* and in the *Passion* of St. Simeon.[2] It is not reasonable to suppose that the evangelization of the northern regions had proceeded from Seleucia-Ctesiphon.

---

[1] *Acta Martyrum*, Bedjan, t. I, Leipzig, 1890, pp. 86 ff.

[2] There is a manifest difference in the theology reflected in the *Martyrium* and that of the *Narratio*. The former is much nearer to the thought and feeling of Aph.' *Homilies*.

To summarize the evidence above, it may be said that the Christianity of Mesopotamia came probably from Edessa, and that the original missionaries and their northern converts as well, were of the Jewish people. The introduction of Christianity took place not far from the beginning of the third century at the latest, as is indicated both by the Asianic Christology of Aphraates and the presence of so many Jewish elements in the form and substance of his thought. That the constituency of the Persian Church in the north was Judeo-Christian originally, and that it never quite lost the character given to it at the beginning, seems to be shown by the relations between it and Judaism. Aphraates understood the Jews, while he would have had considerable difficulty in understanding the point of view of his co-religionists of Rome or Antioch. This intimacy in thought had its dangers, for the Christians of the north were few in number; and while they were no menace to the Jews, the latter were, especially in times of persecution, a cause of much anxiety to the Christians. Aphraates' solicitude for his co-religionists and his fear of the effect on them of Jewish polemics, is not of the same sort as the bitterness against the Jews shown in the *Acta* recording contemporaneous events, for this was inspired by the attitude of the Jews toward the persecuted Christians.[1]

III. THE JEWS UNDER THE SASSANIDS.

The position of the Jews at this time was on the whole not unfavorable. There were settlements of Jews in northern Mesopotamia at a very early date. R. Jehuda ben Batera, the account of whose journey to Nisibis is told in the Midrash *Echa Rabbati*,[2] took up his abode there, after studying under R. Eli'ezer ben Hyrkanos in Palestine.[3] He belonged to the second generation of Tannaim,

---

[1] 992 : 1 — 18, and 993 : 1 — 7, give Aphraates' interview with a "man called ܠܝܘܩܝ ܚܟܝܡܐ and is typical of the relation between Jews and Christians. The ܚܟܝܡܐ quotes St. Mt. 17¹⁹, 21²¹ to Aph. apropos of the powerlessness of the Christians in the face of persecution.

[2] Midrash Rabba, *sepher D'barim*, (Warsaw ed. Levin Epstein, vol. V) on איכה ר', 3, p. טו pp. 51—2.

[3] Of whom R. Jochanan ben Zakkai said that he was בור סוד שאינו מאבד טפה in *Pirke Aboth* 2¹¹ and cf. ff. about him.

and is reckoned the eighth of the second group.[1] This "generation," according to Mielziner, extends over the year 80—120. According to Talmudic references, Berliner dates R. Jehuda ben Batera "shortly after the destruction of the second Temple."[2] There are many allusions to R. Jehuda, which suggest that his work in establishing the school at Nisibis was not in vain.[3] Before R. Simlai went south to Nehardea he had first taught at Nisibis.[4] He had come to Nisibis from Lydda and was "reputed less for his teachings as a teacher of the Halacha than for his ingenious and lucid method of treating the Agada."[5] He was really of the first generation of Palestinian Amoraim (219—279) and was one of the links between Palestine and Babylonia.[6] His association at Nisibis was with the school begun there by R. Jehuda ben Batera, which was still flourishing.[6] Other notes on the city of Nisibis in Jewish history make it highly probable that it was from the earliest time a centre of scholarly education and instruction, and that its school endured at least into the time of the greatest of the Sassanids.[7] The city of Nisibis had been Roman territory since Trajan Parthicus had recaptured it in 115, till in 194 the Osrhoenians took it. The Roman colony, established unser Septimius Severus, held it for Rome and it was well fortified. Nisibis was the subject of constant disputes between Rome and Persia, until under the weakest of the Sassanids, Narses I, it was acquired by Rome again (297). After this for a period of twelve years beginning in 350, Sapur II three times besieged it in vain, till in 363 it was finally ceded to the

---

[1] Thus Mielziner, (*Intro. to Talmud*) pp. 25—27; Strack, (*Einleitung in den Talmud*), p. 92, who refers to W. Bacher, *Agada der Tannaiten*, Straßburg, 1903, pp. 378—385, Fränkel, Brüll, etc.

[2] By reference to *Sanhedrin 32ᵇ*, cf. A. Berliner, *Beiträge zur Geographie und Ethnographie Babyloniens im Talmud und Midrash*, (Berlin, 1884), pp. 53—54.

[3] cf. A. Hyman, *Sepher Toledoth Tannaim ve Amoraim*, London, 1910. vol. 2 pp. 555—557, where they are given in full, as also in *Sepher Seder Haddoroth* ed. S Heilprin, (Warsaw, 1882) vol. II, pp. 163—165.

[4] *Aboda Zara*, 36ᵃ, with which cf Talmud Jer. Aboda Zara, II, 8.

[5] Mielziner, *op. cit.*, p. 43.

[6] cf. *Sepher Tol. Tan. v. Amor.* (Hyman) vol. III, pp. 1150—1152, s. v.

[7] Hirschensohn, *Sepher Sheva Hochmoth*, (London, 1912) s. v. נציבין page קצא and especially the note (הערה).

[8] Dion Cassius, LXVIII, 23.

Persians on the defeat by them of the forces of Julian.[1] It was on the trade route from the West to Mosul, by which both Jew and Christian could travel easily from Syria to northern Mesopotamia.

Besides the indigenous population of Jews, who had through good and evil days maintained their identity and national life since the exile, and, from the second Christian century onward, had at their head a "Resh G'lutha,"[2] the Jewish population of "Babylon" had been augmented by the coming in of exiles from Palestine. The outcome of the rebellion of Simeon bar Chozeba (called „Bar Cocheba" — 132—134) had sent still more Jews into "Babylon," who came from the Roman domains into the country of the Parthians and Sassanids in ever increasing numbers with every new act of hostility launched against them. Gradually "Babylonia became for the Jewish nation a second mother."[3] The Jews had their own political chief, the Resh G'lutha,[4] and their obligations to the Persian government were satisfied by the payment of taxes and imposts.[5] In other respects they had in Persia that which they were denied by Rome, — autonomy and religious liberty. Conditions under the early Christian emperors were peculiarly

[1] ibid., LXXV, 23. When it was ceded to the Persians it was an important Christian centre. The see of Nisibis was founded by Babu (ob. 309). cf. J. B. Chabot, L'école de Nisibe: son histoire, ses Status, (Paris, 1896). Guidi, Gli Statuti della Scuola di Nisibi, (in Giornale della Società asiatica italiana, IV, pp. 165—195).

[2] s. v. "Israel," (in Encycl. Brit., American issue, ninth edition, Chicago, 1892, vol. XIII) by Julius Wellhausen, p. 429; Graetz, Gesch. d. Süd., vol. II, p. 133—134.

[3] Graetz, Gesch. d. Juden, Leipzig, 1888, vol. II, p. 131. On the history of the Jews from the time of Hadrian through that of the early Christian emperors, and in both the west and in Persia, cf. pp. 75—183, ibid.

[4] According to Graetz, op. cit., et vol. cit., p. 133, he ranked the fourth in the Persian kingdom. This Nöldeke (Tabari, p. 68) thinks very doubtful.

[5] Graetz, op. et vol. cit., p. 133. It was on account of his refusal to pay this sort of tribute, or perhaps rather the double tribute that Sapur exacted of all in order to furnish means to carry on his war against Rome, that Simeon b. Sabba'e was indicted and his arrest ordered. cf. Martyrium, St. Sim. b. Sab., sec. 10, and Narratio ibid., secs. 9, 10, (Patrol. Syr., pars prima, t. II, cols. 731—734 and 802—803, 806). If Sapur had tried to make him equal to the גלותא ריש and Simeon had until this time enjoyed Sapur's favor, it would seem that this account in both MS₁ and MS₂ cannot be true to the facts; for discussion, cf. Kmosko, Patrol. Syr., pars prima, vol. II, pp. 705—709 (sec. 8 of Praefatio III). St. Simeon bar Sabba'e is called ܠܒܝ ܠܒ; cf. ibid. 799:14; 818:13; 867:23.

unhappy for the Jews. "Judaism would have rejoiced in the victory of the Spirit over the power of arms had victorious Christianity really carried out in practice the meekness of its Founder."[1] Constantine's edict of toleration (312—313) soon proved a dead letter, for any proselytism of Christians was forbidden. Jews were not allowed in Jerusalem, except on the day of the commemoration of its loss. Under Constantius, persecution was very bitter, and many Jews went to Babylonia. Marriage between Jew and Christian had been forbidden under pain of death (339). Roman legislation had prohibited the holding of Christian slaves by Jews.[2] The argument employed by way of trying to win Jews from their faith ran somewhat as follows: "Why do you kill yourselves for your God? See how many punishments are inflicted upon you, how much you suffer in the way of confiscation of your goods! Cmoe to us, and we will make you counts, nobles and peers." It is instructive to compare with this[3] the argument of the Jew which Aphraates reports in his twenty-first homily.[4] In both cases the opponent reasons that that religious allegiance must be defective which involves persecution and suffering on the part of those most devoted to it. In the whole of the twenty-first homily Aphraates attempts to refute this argument, and to comfort and strengthen his brothers in the Christian Faith.[5]

The great school cities of Babylonia were now flourishing. Abba Arikha,[6] („Rab") a noble Babylonian, went to study with his uncle, R. Chiya, in Palestine, and completed his studies under R. Jehuda Hannasi. After the latter's death[7] he returned to his homeland, and founded the academy at Sura. (219 A. D.) As the sayings of over a hundred of his disciples[8] are recorded in

---

[1] Graetz, *op. et vol. cit.*, p. 159.

[2] *ibid.*, pp. 161—166.

[3] from Graetz. *op. et vol cit.*, p. 162.

[4] 932 : 8 — 18.

[5] vide homily XX', especially sec. 21.

[6] רב ערוך בחון *Nidda* 24b — quoted in Bacher, *Agada d. babyl. Amor.* He was of lofty stature, — a noble in appearance as well as in lineage and character.

[7] As to the time of his return, — whether some years before the foundation of the academy at Sura, or just before that event, cf. Strack, *Einleitung*, pp. 100—101.

[8] Mielziner, *op. cit.*, p. 44.

the Talmud he can well be said to have obeyed the command
of the men of the "Great Synagogue" — הרבה תלמידים העמידו.[1]
He gave a great impetus to the development of *haggada*, though
it is doubtful whether a collection of haggadic material was really
made in his day. As a bridge between the Tannaim and Amoraim
he is held to have had the right to dispute precepts of the Mishnah.[2]
He died in 247 (A. D.).[3]

There are two towns named Sura mentioned in Rabbinic
literature.[4] The Sura where Rab founded his academy lay on
the west shore of the Euphrates, on an estuary, a good day's
journey from Nehardea, and on lower ground than the latter.[5] It
was west from Pumbeditha. Neither in Nehardea nor in Sura
were there any Christians.[6] The work of Rab, besides being conspicuous for the large number of disciples he had gathered, made
him eminent as a haggadist, who created and discovered new
methods,[7] while the content of his haggada may have been
handed down by tradition. He employed the allegorical method
very little.[8] One of his methods was to compare the several
possible meanings of a term, and another is that called "gematria."
Bacher calls attention to the fact that the best developed and
favorite element in *haggada*, the parable, was almost never used
by Rab.[9] His was a conspicuously original type of genius.[10]

The city of Nehardea was in constant communication with
Palestine[11] until in 260 it was destroyed by Odenatus of Palmyra,[12]

---

[1] Pirke *Aboth.*, i. ib.

[2] תנא הוא ופליג: *Erub.* 50b; *Baba Bathra* 42a, *Sanh.* 83b.

[3] Bacher, *Agada d. babyl. Am.*, p. 45.

[4] Berliner, *Beiträge zur Geographie*, p. 55.

[5] Berliner, *op. cit.,* p. 51.

[6] *Ber.* 12a, cf. Berliner, *op. cit.,* pp. 49, 56.

[7] W. Bacher, *op. cit.*

[8] *ibid*, p. 30, note 199, where the few instances of the use of this method are given.

[9] Only two instances are ascertainable, — cf. *op. cit.,* p. 31, and note 203.

[10] On his life, cf. M. J. Mühlfelder, *Rabh; Ein Lebensbild zur Geschichte des
Talmuds*, Leipzig, 1871; and Strack *op. cit.,* p. 101, where other references are given.

[11] Berliner, *op. cit.,* pp. 50—56. Intercourse with Palestine viâ Nehardea was
never so constant and so free as in the days of the first two generations of Amorain,
cf. Bacher, *op. cit.,* pp. 85 ff.

[12] cf. W. Wright, *Palmyra & Zenobia*, 1896.

who in that year proclaimed himself king, and began a campaign against the Persian empire which brought him eventually into alliance with Rome. His real campaign against Sapur began in 265,[1] when both in his own pretended right as an independent sovereign and also as subject of the Roman empire, he made inroads into the Persian state, which caused alarm and distress everywhere that his arms or his fame reached. To Odenatus the Jews applied the words of Dan. 7[8].[2] Three years before the destruction of this city, of which the population of Jews must have opposed Odenatus as an expression of hostility against Rome and of that loyalty to Persia which Mar Samuel had engendered, Mar Samuel had died. He had succeeded R. Sheila as *Resh Sidra* in that city, after having studied in Palestine. R. Sheila had used the haggadic method of teaching,[3] and his successor, Mar Samuel, continued to develop it. Examples of his *haggada* are found in the controversies between him and Rab, his friend. They used much the same method, but differed as to conclusions.[4] With Rab he agreed in denouncing asceticism.[5] Perhaps his conspicuous doctrine, with special relation to the subject matter of the present essay, is the principle which he enunciated that the civil law of the government is as valid for the Jews as their own law.[6] He was superior to the great Rab in civil law.[7] It was doubtless owing to his influence that certain conciliatory measures were adopted out of deference to the fanaticism of the Magi and their prescriptions regarding the use of fire, etc. This counsel allowed the Jews to bend gracefully beneath the storm of Zoroastrian

---

[1] According to the chronology of W. Robertson Smith in *Encycl. Brit.* (Am. issue) ninth ed., 1892, vol. XVIII, p. 201, note 2.

[2] Graetz, *op. cit. et vol. cit.*, p. 144. Graetz's date for the destruction of Nehardea is 259.

[3] Bacher, *op. cit.*, pp. 5—7.

[4] *ibid.*, pp. 37—40.

[5] *Taan.* 11[a]. *Nedar* 22[a], and cf. note 46, p. 41, cf. Bacher, *op. cit.*

[6] Mielziner, *op. cit.*, p. 44. The sentence דינא דמלכותא דינא *Baba Bathra* 55[a], is to be interpreted in the light of his teaching regarding the relation between the omnipotent power of the heavenly "Kingdom" (*i. e.*, "Rule") and the earthly power, which determined his whole attitude toward rule of the government under which he was, — cf. *Baba Bathra*, 3[b], *Arachin*, 6[a]; Bacher, *op. cit.*, p. 44—45, note 70.

[7] הלכתא כרב באיסורי וכשמואל בדינין: *Bechoroth* 49[b].

intolerance in the "New Persia" of the beginning of the Sassanid
dynasty. The Christians, who evidently were incapable of such
yielding and concessions, suffered extremely, especially in the cities
of upper Mesopotamia, — the environs of Nisibis, and in Edessa,
where they were by this time (226) firmly established, according
to Graetz.[1] The same loyalty to the new government, transition
to which, however, was not always so easy,[2] brought upon the
Jews of Nehardea the wrath of Odenatus, as has been mentioned.
This destruction of Nehardea is never mentioned in the Talmud,
and Odenatus is there called פפא בן נצר[3]. R. Nachunan, who followed
R. Samuel, was the head of the academy at the time of this great
calamity.[4] Of the learned men associated with Nehardea, by far
the most famous is R. Samuel,[5] the impress of whose teaching
was so widely extended and deep. The city itself lay on the
N'har Malka, was the seat of the *Resh G'lutha,*[6] and was one
of the two *loci* on the circumference of Jewish "Babylonia," of
which the second great seat of Jewish life at the other extreme
on the East was Sura.[7]

After the destruction of Nehardea the court moved to Machuza.[8]
Machuza was situated on the Tigris, not far from Nehardea, and
on the *N'har Malka.*[9] The Jews had there the protection of a
large Persian garrison,[10] which was, however, as much of an

---

[1] *op. et vol. cit.,* p. 142; on p. 143 Graetz asserts that Sapur I had been friendly
with Mar S.

[2] cf. the words of Rab upon the death of Artaban, p. 143, Graetz, *op. cit.*

[3] Berliner, *op. cit.,* p. 51.

[4] cf. *Erubin* 34[b] and *Gittin* 45[a].

[5] An excellent monograph on him is S. D. Hoffmann's *Mar Samuel, Lebensbild
eines talmudischen Weisen der ersten Hälfte des dritten Jahrhunderts,* Leipzig, 1873;
cf. also on Mar Samuel in *Hayye Hayehudim bizeman Hattalmud, sepher Nehardea,*
S. Judilwitz, Wilna, 1905, pp. 30—47; *Toleaoth Tannaim ve Amoraim,* vol. III,
pp. 1120—1131; *Seder hoddoroth Tannaim ve Amoraim,* vol. II, pp. 352 ff., Strack,
Einleitung, p. 101, and accompanying references.

[6] *Baba Bathra* 36[a].

[7] On the geography of the cities, cf. s. v. נהרדעא in Hirschensohn, *Sheva Choch-
moth,* pp. 164—166; Berliner, *op. cit.,* pp. 47—51; in *Hayye Hayyehudim bizeman
Hattalmud, sepher Nehardea,* by S. Judilwitz (Wilna, 1905), pp. 1—29.

[8] cf. *Sheva Hochmoth,* pp. 155—157.

[9] cf. Berliner, *op. cit.,* pp. 51—52.

[10] *Sab.* 147[b]; *Taanith.* 21[a].

embarrassment as a benefit to them. Raba could not extend his customary invitation to all who were in need to come in and eat, lest he be swamped by the acceptance of his hospitality on the part of all of the soldiers of the garrison who might accept![1] There were many proselytes, whose morals were not of the best. The town suffered from its prosperity, in that temporal well-being induced spiritual laxity. It lay near to Seleucia, the capital of Sapur II, and was thus at the centre of the life of the Persian empire.[2] While Rab Shesheth removed there from Nehardea after the destruction of that city,[3] he left it shortly to found his school at Silḥi. The great glory of Machuza, among the first three generations of Amoraim, was Raba (299—352). He had studied with R. Nachman and R. Ḥisda, and later under Rabba bar Nachmani. R. Abaye at Pumbaditha (see below) was his rival, but Raba's superior genius drew crowds of disciples to Machuza. Under these two, dialectics reached its greatest development. His public lectures and disputations are more frequently related than those of any other Babylonian. A long *midrash* on Esther at the end of the tractate *Megillah* (10b—17a) is his work or that of his disciple, as is that on Lamentations in *Sanhedrin* 104a ff.[4] By the time of Raba, wealth and prosperity had increased greatly. The poor were sharply divided from the rich.[5] A similar separation between learned and unlearned, which distinction did not exist under the Tannaim, had also become a fact. Scholars had developed into a caste and had come to speak of the study of the Law as an end in itself.[6] Thus the common people said of them: "What good are these scholars? They accumulate learning for themselves only!"[7] Such, R. Joseph denounced as "heretics."[7] Learned as Raba was, he had little

---

[1] Berliner, *op. cit.*, p. 40.

[2] cf. the reference in the *Nar. St. Sim. b. S. Patrol.*, *Syr.*, pars I, t. II, 810 : 22, and Kmosko's note (2).

[3] *Sepher Toledoth T. v. A.*, vol. III, pp. 1231—1233; and on his residence in Shechanzib, cf. Berliner, *op. cit.*, pp. 64—65. He had studied under Mar Samuel. On his *haggada* cf. Bacher, *op. cit.*, pp. 76—79.

[4] Mielziner, *op. cit.*, p. 50.

[5] Thus Bacher, *op. cit.*, p. 119—121.

[6] As did, *e. g.*, R. Joseph; *Meg.* 16b, *Sota* a, Nidda 61b.

[7] *Sanhedrin* 99b; and cf. Graetz, *op. cit.*, p. 176.

patience with the people of Machuza, who were mostly proselytes. He was of pure Jewish strain and of a noble family. The virtues of humility, meekness, and unselfishness were not conspicuously displayed in his character.[1] He had to maintain his standing with Sapur II by the payment of heavy tribute. When a man, convicted of a criminal offence according to the Jewish law (which Raba administered), was by his order flogged, and died, it was only the Queen Mother's intercession with her son that stayed Sapur's wrath.[2] The Queen Mother, Ephra Hormiz, was throughout partial to the Jews, as is shown by her gifts of money to R. Joseph,[3] and to Raba. Other gifts, as of sacrificial animals,[4] were doubtless an embarrassment, save in so far as they assured the Jews of her goodwill.[5] It is scarcely to be wondered at that Raba complains: "We have always been the servants of Ahasuerus."[6] On Lev. 13[13] instead of כֻּלּוֹ הָפַךְ לָבָן he reads the words: כולו הפך לבֶּן, to give foundation for R. Isaac's statement that "the Messiah would come when Rome became Christian."[7] It was probably not a mere interest in the fact which prompted him to say that Rome was more powerful than Persia,[8] with his precarious tenure of the royal favor.

Next only to Nehardea and Sura in importance was the academy of Pumbeditha, where there was a community of Jews and a synagogue at the time of Rab.[9] The town lay near Nehardea at the mouth of the canal named בדיתא. Its inhabitants enjoyed no good reputation,[10] but its renown was based upon the generations of great scholars who taught there. R. Jehuda bar Jecheskel, the

---

1 cf. Graetz, *op. et vol. cit.*, pp. 174—178.

2 *Taanith* 24[b]. In spite of this, Raba did not escape the wrath of public opinion. Cf. Graetz, p. 177.   3 *Baba Qama* 8[a].

4 *Zebachim* 116[a], and cf. *Nid.* 20[b].

5 The *Acta Martyrum* accuse her of conspiring with the Jews to incite her son to persecute them. This Duval (*La lit. Syriaque*, p. 134) rejects and Funk (*Die haggadischen Elemente in den Homilien des Aphraates*, p. 11) denies. For a discussion of her relations with Jews and Christians, cf. *Pat. Syr.*, pars I, t. *II*, pp. 693—694, where Kmosko has collected all the evidence.

6 *Megilla*, 14[a].

7 *Sanhed.* 97[a].

8 *Shevuoth* 6[a].

9 *Sab.* 110[a].

10 cf. Berliner, *op. cit.*, pp. 57—58.

"acute,"[1] founded its academy, after studying under Rab at Sura and Mar Samuel at Nehardea. He was a contemporary of Rab Huna (212—297) who succeeded Mar Samuel at Sura in 257. At Rab Huna's death he followed him as ריש מתיבתא at Sura, dying two years later.[2] Under Rabba bar Nachmani (270—330, called "Rabba") who had studied under the Sura scholars, Rab Huna, Rab Juda, and Rab Ḥisda, the academy at Pumbeditha flourished. His authorship of the Palestinian *Midrash* to Genesis is denied by Bacher, on excellent grounds, since of recorded haggadic sayings attributed to him there are very few indeed.[3] Between Rabba and Rab Joseph (who succeeded him in 330, and only held office for three years), there was a deep friendship, based on mutual respect and the supremacy of each in his own field. Rabba was called the "uprooter of mountains,"[4] and Rab Joseph "Sinai."[5] The former was eminent as a dialectician, the latter conspicuous for his knowledge about and exposition of the sources of the Law. R. Joseph worked on the Targum of the Bible, and translated and published the prophets in the vernacular.[6] His primary devotion was to the text of the Bible rather than to deductions from it in the dialectic manner of Rabba. Very little haggadic material of either has come down to us . . His employment of the parable — as, *e. g.,* in *Nidda* 31[a] — is worthy of note especially because of the rarity of its use by the Babylonians. He valued the study of the Law more than works of piety.[7]

Rabba had gathered a great number of students about him, and the flourishing academy of Pumbeditha with its more than one thousand students attracted the unfavorable attention of enemies of the Jews. It was said that many of his students attended his lectures in order to evade the poll tax, and, since he was charged

---

[1] שמואל קרא אותו שינגא: *Berach.* 37ᵃ.

[2] cf. *Sepher Seder Haddoroth*, vol. II, pp, 179—181.

3 Bacher, *op. cit.,* pp. 98—99.

[4] *Berach.* 64ᵃ, *Hor.* 14ᵃ, — cf. Bacher, p. 101, notes 1 and 2; on his life, works, sayings, disciples. etc., cf. *Sepher Toledoth Tan. v. Am.,* vol. III, pp. 1062—1070.

5 cf. *Seph. Toledoth,* vol. II, pp. 742—749, especially p. 745.

6 Graetz, *op. et vol. cit.,* p. 172.

7 cf. Bacher, *op. cit.,* pp. 104—106.

with conniving at this, Rabba fled, and died in solitude (330).[1]
This kind of hostility was, however, not altogether uncommon, in
spite of the favor of the Queen Mother who sent a generous
offering after Rabba's death to his successor, R. Joseph.[2] The
story is told of Rabba bar bar Chana,[3] (who had studied under
R. Jochanan bar Napacha[4] (199—279) at Tiberias, and had returned
to his native land to propagate his teacher's methods and precepts)
that during an illness R. Juda and his pupil Rabba visited him.
It was on the festival of Ormuzd on which the Jews were not
allowed lights,[5] and a "geber" (= "fire priest") came in and ex-
tinguished the lamp while they were talking. Thereupon Rabba
b. b. Chana cried out: "Either let us dwell under Thy protection,
(= let us not live) — or at least under the protection of the
children of Esau" (Rome).[6] This kind of petty inconvenience,
however, did not disguise or alter the great fact that in the main
the Jews under Sapur II were far better off than their fellow-
countrymen under Roman rule. The Queen Mother's kind offices
doubtless availed often to soften prejudice and remove the disa-
bilities which the hostile priests of Zoroaster desired to place
upon the practice of any religion but their own.

Under Rab Abaye[7] Nachmani (280—338), who succeeded
R. Joseph at Pumbeditha, the glory of the latter academy waned
in the brilliance of Machuza, which attracted many pupils under
Raba's[8] leadership. Contrary opinions of the two are almost always
coupled together in the Talmud, but in practical matters Rabba's
opinion almost always prevailed, only six instances to the contrary

---

[1] Graetz, *op. cit.*, p. 171—172, cf. *Baba Metzia*, 86ª.

[2] *Baba Qama* 8ª.

[3] Son of Abba bar Chana, not as Graetz makes him, R. b. Chana; cf. Bacher
op. cit., p. 87, note (5).

[4] cf. *Sepher Toledoth Tan. v. Am.*, vol. II, pp. 652—672.

[5] Bacher, *op. cit.*, p. 87, note 4.

[6] *Gittin* 16:1.

[7] *Sepher Seder Haddoroth*, vol. II, pp. 22—25; *Sepher Toledoth Tan. v. Am.*,
vol. I, pp. 74—87.

[8] Abba bar Abba said to his pupils: "Instead of gnawing at the bones served
up to you in the academy of Abaye, go and eat meat at Raba's school," (*Baba
bathra* 22ª); on the text and its emendation, cf. *op. cit.*, Bacher, pp. 108—109,
note 7.

being noted.[1] His principles of interpretation are of considerable interest,[2] being in many ways a reaction against the contemporary dialectic. Of the early fourth century Amoraim at Sura, Rab Chisda (219—309) and Rabba bar Huna his successor (died 322), were contemporaries of Rab Abaye and Raba. At the death of Rabba bar Huna the academy at Sura was deserted until the time of Rab Ashe. At the time Aphraates wrote his controversial homilies (344—345), the dominant Jewish school was that of Machuza under Raba, which had now supplanted both Pumbeditha and Sura, Sura, in its turn, having yielded the palm to Pumbeditha under the presidency of Rab Joseph and Abaye Nachmani. The great throngs of Jews from all over Babylonia which attended Raba's lectures must have carried his teaching far and wide. To him, as has been said, are ascribed the two *Midrashim* on Esther and Lamentations He was an eminent haggadist who employed the haggadic method very largely, though he did not reject the popular proverb.[3] The Jews enjoyed a comparatively quiet and untroubled existence under the Sassanids from the time of Mar Samuel on. The difficulties they experienced from time to time were a sharp lesson. The moral to be drawn from each clash between the Jews and the government was merely the rediscovery of the truth of Mar Samuel's dictum that the civil law of the government should be accepted as the civil law of the Jews.[4] The conciliatory attitude which he adopted served as a *modus vivendi*. Every violation of his principle only proved its value both theoretically und practically.

IV. The Homilies of Aphraates in relation to Jewish thought

Conditions of Jews and Christians During the Persecution compared

For the Christian there was no such way out. Even under the loose government of the oriental dynasty of the Sassanids,[5] the

---

[1] *Baba Metzia* 21[b]; *Sanhedrin* 27[a]; *Erubin* 15[a]; *Kidd* 52[a]; *Gittin* 34[a].
[2] cf. Bacher, *op. cit.*, pp. 112—113.   [3] cf. Bacher, *op. cit.*, p. 123.
[4] *Baba Bathra* 55[a].
[5] On its organization cf. Nöldeke's *Tabari*, pp. 102, 436—458; and Labourt's *Le Christianisme dans l'empire perse*, pp. 1—9.

measure of autonomy which the Christians enjoyed in the north and in Seleucia, only made them restive. A state under Christian rule, with the Church fully recognized and supreme in her own domain, was the only ideal worth living for.[1] The condition of the Church under the Sassanids was tolerable only as an *interim* stage. When persecution broke out against them the real issue was revealed. Rome was the Christian state, and its ruler, who took counsel always with the Bishops whom he constantly had with him and held in high reverence, the means for delivering captive Christians, exiles in a foreign and hostile land. The prophecies of the exile were perhaps more luminous with meaning for Christians than for the Jews of their day.[2] The Christians had no friend at court like Iphra Hormiz. Theoretically they could not feel justified in admitting a compromise. When by reason of political exigencies and the necessities of his campaign Sapur demanded a loyal cooperation in waging the war against Rome, his Christian subjects did not give it. In the fifth homily of Aphraates we see the attitude of mind which provoked persecution.[3] If Raba thought Rome more powerful than Persia,[4] and Rabba bar bar Chana fretfully wished for Roman domination as a relief from the petty inconveniences of Persian rule,[5] Aphraates openly expressed his views in no uncertain terms. „That kingdom of the children of Esau will not be given over to the forces now gathered which are coming up against it, for it (now) guards the kingdom for Him who has given it, and He it is who protects it."[6] The reason that Roman power had not yet conquered Persia is that Rome did not carry Him

[1] In homily XXIII Aphraates had seemingly come to despair of this ideal being realized in his day, and his vision became entirely "otherworldly" (cf. II:144:19—25, and the whole of Sec. 67). This is not necessarily an inconsistency, since the failure of a concrete human hope would not alter the fundamentally supernatural cast of his ideals, but, rather, bring them into sharper prominence.

[2] cf. the list of quotations from the prophets, references, and occasions, in Parisot's ed., vol. II, pp. 482 - 484.

[3] cf. especially secs. 1, 3, 13, 23—25.

[4] *Shevuoth* 6ª.

[5] *Gittin* 16ᵇ.

[6] Aph. 233 : 12—15

in their midst by whom the victory was to be won.[1] Now that Rome is Christian the designs of God are to be carried out. Rome is now a fit instrument for God to use in the fulfilment of his own prophecy. Aphraates claims to build this certain forecast on the words of St. Luke 14[11], alleging that it is consistent with God's previous ways of working in mankind. Persia (he felt in 336—337) was certainly doomed to defeat at the hands of Rome.

Common Elements in Aphraates and Contemporary Judaism: the Same Envisagement of Religion.

Once persecution had broken out, many difficulties beset the Christians. In the districts where the persecutions were not organized, (for in the early years there were only local outbreaks, and it was but for a comparatively short time that there was a systematic persecution all over the Empire,[2]) there were many things to fear: apostasy[3] into a formal adherence to the government religion; despair[4] and lapse into irreligion, and even a lapse into Judaism.[5] Aphraates' "controversial" homilies show that the danger of lapsing into Judaism was the occasion and reason for their being written. They are written primarily for Christians,[6] with a special view to providing Aphraates' fellow-believers with the necessary defence against Jewish attack. Their object was not to convert Jews, but to roll back the danger with which the Christians were being beset. The Jewish argument was cogent. Christian and Jew had the same one God. Christian and Jew recognized the same Old Testament and used the same text (the

---

[1] cf. latter part of sec. 23 of the fifth homily.

[2] cf. La Christianisme dans l'empire Perse, pp. 56—86; De persecutione Saporis, being chapter III of the Preface to St. Simeon bar Sabba'e, by M. Kmosko, in Pat. Syr., Pars I, t. II, pp. 690—713.

[3] cf. Le Christianisme, p. 62.

[4] The chief of Arewan bought his freedom at the price of slaying with his own hands the monk Badema; cf. Acta Martyr. Orientalium, ed. St. Ev. Assemani, Rome, 1748, vol. I, p. 167. Abdisho, Bishop of a town near Kaska, was betrayed by his nephew, ibid., p. 152.

[5] That this was a real possibility is seen from sec. 22 of the Narratio de St. Simeon b. Sab., cf. Pat. Syr., pars I, t. II, col. 823.

[6] cf. 489:19 - 20; 528:8 — 9; 532:19 — 24; 533:21 — 24; 540:2 — 4; 568:6 — 10; 572:20 — 23; homily 15, sec. 1, 744:15 — 20; 757:12 — 15, etc.

Peshitto).[1] If some of the members of the church of Aphraates
had been Jews, a return to their original faith would not be difficult, especially under the conditions of the time when Jews were
comparatively free from the sort of persecution to which the
Christians were exposed. If the condition of convert Jews in the
Christian communities of Persia was so unhappy, because of
the pressure of Persian persecutions and the none too friendly
attitude of the Jews, exempt as they were from the official
disfavor which had fallen upon the Christians,—the lot of Persian
Gentile converts was still harder. Persian Christians felt the force
of the demands of loyalty to the Persian emperor, since all were
of the same blood. Furthermore, the Latin and the Persian were
natural enemies. Judaism offered a compromise, for it would
be a great advance over their former paganism. They could
still be monotheists; they could retain their ethical standards, and
their religion would be of the same general type as Christianity.
By becoming proselytes of Judaism they could in a measure save
their consciences and, at the same time, clear themselves of the
stigma of disloyalty to their own government and declare themselves on the side of their fellow-countrymen against the hated
foreigner.

The strong common bonds between Judaism and the Christianity of the Church of Aphraates made a reversion to Judaism not
at all difficult. His Christianity was envisaged in the same terms
as Judaism. One cannot but notice that the two religions were
of the same quality. No alien philosophy was interlocked with
his theology, so that the two could not be separated. Perhaps
the greatest distinctively Christian element in his theology was
Aphraates' doctrine of the Sacraments. But it was no such
doctrine as could be aligned with the type of sacramental teaching
of the heathen mystery religions; it was predominantly ethical.[2]

---

[1] It was a contemporary of Aphraates who translated the prophets into the
vernacular Aramaic — Rab Joseph (ob. 333). cf. Graetz, *Gesch., op. et vol. cit.,*
p. 171.

[2] On his ethical teaching, cf. 137:1—2; 473:19—23; 313:1—3, 13—16,
353:11—15; 168:23—28; 29:12—15; II:128:18—21; II:129:9—10; 180:
18—21; 172:5—14; 173:14—15; 920:12—14; 572:14—15; 113:6—11; and IX,
sec. 10,

The Jews looked for a Messiah; Aphraates said that this Messiah had already come.[1] The Jews held that the Messiah should be such as to fulfill all prophecies;[2] Aphraates taught that all Christian teachings, practices, and dogmas had their type in the Old Testament. As Jesus was foreshadowed by many great worthies of the Old Testament,[3] so the ordinances of the New Covenant were related as fulfilment, or antitype, to the "types" found in the Old.[4] Thus Circumcision, the type, gave way to its fulfilment,[5] Baptism; the Passover, to the Eucharist;[6] the כנסת ישראל to the Church;[7] the Law, to the Gospel. Christianity was essentially the flowering of the plant Judaism. He could not conceive of the New Testament without the Old,—the Gospel without the Law: Fulfilment without Prophecy.[8] It is worthy of note that just those sides of Pauline teaching appeal to Aphraates' thought as had reference to the relation of Jesus to the prophecies,[9] of the Church to Israel,[10] of Christian ordinances to their types in the O.T.;[11] only such elements of Pauline teaching were really assimilated and thoroughly digested.[12] It is just where

---

[1] Homily XVII, "That the Messiah is the Son of God," is "against the Jews" (785 : 1—2) and especially secs. 9—12.

[2] 804 : 7—25; 805 : 1—27; 813 : 6—25.

[3] 813 : 6—25; Jacob's vision, a foreshadowing of Jesus the Messiah, cf. 148 : 1—4; XI sec. 12; Jacob, XXI, sec. 9; Moses, sec. 10, etc., all as prophetic types of Jesus.

[4] The contrast in Aph. is between ܐܪܙܐ and ܩܘܫܬܐ. ܐܪܙܐ = "mystery" (also in sense of "sacrament.")   [5] cf. Homily XI, sec. 12.

[6] "The mystery (ܐܪܙܐ) (of the Passover) was given to the Former People, (i. e. the Jews) but its fulfilment (lit., "truth" = ܩܘܫܬܐ) to-day is preached among the Gentiles". (516 : 4—5).

[7] II : 40 : 10—13; II : 92 : 12—15; Hom. XXI, sec. 20, the ܟܢܘܫܬܐ ܕܥܡܐ 765 : 4—5.

[8] There are almost twice as many quotations from the Old, as from the New Testament: approximately 1056 to 564 instances of explicit quotation.

[9] The "Diatessaron", which Aph. used with the addition of the genealogical passages, is based upon the first Gospel. It would not have been uncongenial to Aph. that the bulk of that Gospel, which aims at displaying the eminent character of Jesus as Fulfiller of prophecy, should be incorporated into the Diatessaron.   [10] Cf. Rom. 9 6; I Cor. 10 18; Gal. 6 16.

[11] Rom. 4 11, 12; Gal. 5 2, 5, 6; 6 12, 13, 15; Col. 2 11, 12 3 11; Eph. 2 11; Phil. 3 3; I Cor. 10 2, 12 13; Gal. 3 27; Rom. 6 3, 4; Heb. 6 2, etc.

[12] For example, there is no strong indication of any appreciation of the characteristic Pauline doctrine of "justification by faith", though Aph. does use the words·

3

St. Paul functioned as a Jew that Aphraates best understands his thought. The author of the Epistle to the Hebrews, on the other hand, supplied what Aphraates very greatly needed: the theory of the fulfilment of the High Priesthood in Jesus.[1]

Aphraates regarded the Gospels as his *Torah*. The Epistles were an inspired commentary on and interpretation of them. It is not straining the facts to think of him as a kind of interpreter of this *Mishna*,—the Epistles. The very words of the Gospel had both a literal as well as an allegorical or symbolic meaning. Yet he did not base all of his teaching on the text of Scripture. Its interpretation was to be sought for in tradition, and any deduction of an individual were to be aligned with the consensus of living opinion in the Church. Of his doctrine about Jesus,[2] His Person and work, it is sufficient here to say that he thought of Him at least as Messiah in the Jewish meaning of the word.[3] The new Race which had Jesus at its Head stood in a peculiarly intimate relation with God.[4] The bond between the Christian and God was initiated and sustained by the indwelling presence of the Holy Spirit,—the same Holy Spirit which had inspired the Old Testament prophets, and had spoken through them.[5] The Sacraments were the means by which the Holy Spirit was given to the individual.[6] Here he would seem to diverge radically from the Jewish conception of grace and of the gift of the Spirit. But this divergence is not so fundamental, if it be kept in mind that

Cf., s. v. "iustificatio", and "iustus", in "index analyticus" in Parisot's edition. (*Pat. Syr.*, pars I, t, II, p. 456.) His doctrine of "faith" is rather that of Hebrews 11 13—40; cf. Aph. 1009 : 12; 372 : 22—26; 52 : 3—4; 985 : 17—21; 37 : 25—26; cf. I, sec. 18, etc. (Of course, Aph. thought this Epistle to be the work of St. Paul.)

[1] *E. g.*, cf. Hebs. 4 15, Aph. 645 : 21—22 (cf. whole of Hom. XIV, sec. 28); Heb. 9 11, 12, Aph. in Hom. II, sec. 6, 920 : 25—26; Heb. 9 16, 17 also in II : 33 : 2—3; Heb. 10 3, 31 in II : 5 : 2—3, etc.

[2] Cf. Hom. XXII, sec. 26; V, sec. 25; II, sec. 14 (where he says he has been taught by ܡܬܠܐ ܚܒܝܒ : 77 : 9) I, sec. 20; XII, sec. 12.

[3] Cf. Hom. XVII.

[4] Cf. I Cor. 15 44—49 and Aph., 308 : 1—11.

[5] Cf. Heb. 1 1, Aph., Hom. VI, sec. 13 "The Spirit" == "The Holy Spirit" == "the Spirit of Christ" "of which the prophets received" (292 : 13—14). Christians receive this same Spirit (cf. id. sec. 14).

[6] The gift of the Spirit was by Baptism (293 : 2—5, etc.).

in the Law sin was originally conceived of as a kind of infection which could be removed by material means. Similarly holiness might be communicated by these means. Ethical and religious notions were not clearly separated.[1]

While Aphraates says little explicitly about the excellence of the study of Holy Scripture, he everywhere gives evidence of the practice of that principle.[2] Few Christians have shown such a wide and intimate acquaintance with the Bible. Nowhere does he spin a theory or any part of his doctrine out of thin air. One is forced to feel that he was sincerely convinced that every element of his teaching was based on and deduced from the words of Holy Writ. Tradition, as was suggested, had a great share in the development and interpretation of the meaning of Holy Scripture.[3] The Church "of the Gentiles" stood in the same relation to God under the new Christian Dispensation as had Israel under the Old.[4] He felt, in short, that his spiritual ancestors[5] were Abraham, Isaac, Jacob, Moses, Aaron, and the prophets.

There is an excellent commentary in Seeley's *Natural Religion* on the relationship of race to religion. The author points out that the triumph of Christianity is not the victory of certain ideas, so much as "the idealization of the Jewish nationality. It is the extension of the Jewish citizenship to the Gentile. It is this so truly . . . . that the nations of Europe actually adopt as their own the entire history and literature of Israel, so that Jewish traditions, heroes, and poets everywhere supersede the native treasures of memory".[6] Scarcely a more clear case illustrating the action of this principle can be found than that afforded by the *Homilies* of Aphraates. In fact his dependence goes still further than in

---

[1] Cf. G. F. Moore, *History of Religions, vol. II, Judaism, Christianity, Mohammedanism*, New York, Scribner's, 1919, pp. 42—43.

[2] Cf the wide range of his knowledge and the extraordinary number of quotations used by Aph., in Parisot's ed., vol. II (*pars I* of *Pat. Syr.*) Syllabus locorum Sacrae Scripturae, pp. 481—486.

[3] Cf. 77 : 9; etc.

[4] 404 : 12—13; Hom. XVI sec. 3, (765 : 4—5) sec. 5; 980 : 20—22; Hom. XXI, sec. 20, etc.

[5] 468 : 1—5.

[6] 2nd edition (1895), p. 228.

the case of other Gentile or non-Semitic Christian writers. Gentile though he was, Aphraates had adopted for himself all of the spiritual ancestry of Judaism. He did this so thoroughly, and so utterly effaced any traces of allegiance to the spiritual past of his own race, that despite the fact of his non-Jewish nationality[1] (based upon indubitable evidence), he was thoroughly conversant with, and dependent upon Jewish tradition. „Wie vollkommen noch im vierten Jahrhundert die syrische Kirche im Verständnisse des A. T. an die jüdische Tradition gebunden war, zeigen in auffallender Weise die Homilien des Afraats".[2] The extent of this dependence was first suggested in detail by Funk,[3] who gives fifteen instances of haggadic interpretation and illustration of Genesis, eight of Exodus, two of Leviticus, three of Numbers, five of Deuteronomy, and six other instances,—with a doubtful seventh,[4]—of dependence on Aphraates' part, on haggadic material. Parisot adds a number of illustrations of this affiliation with current Jewish tradition.[5]

"No Church father was ever so strongly influenced by rabbinical Judaism as this defender of Christianity against the Jews ... In certain very important questions concerning the soul, God, retribution, etc., he shows himself a docile pupil of the Jews ... His doctrine of the two attributes of God—justice and mercy[6]— is decidedly Jewish ... The oldest rabbinical source is the *Sifre*

---

[1] 789; 19—21; 801 : 6—16; 804: 1—2.

[2] Wellhausen in his edition of Bleek's *Intro. to the O.T.*, vol. IV, (1878), p. 601. quoted by G. Bert in his preface to the translation of Aph. (in Gebhardt u. Harnack, *T. u. U.*, Band III, Heft 3 and 4, 1888, preface pp. VII—XXXVI).

[3] *Die haggadischen Elemente in den Homilien des Aph., des persischen Weisen.* Vienna, 1891, pp. 9—66.

[4] Cf. *op. cit.*, pp. 53—59; on Aph.' doctrine of the "sleep of the soul" (*e. g.*, Aph. 293: 2—25; 296 : 1—26; 297 : 1—6; Hom. XXI, sec. 6, etc.) in which the identity of the Jewish elements has been completely lost, since Aph.' teaching is based upon his own peculiar reading of I Cor. 15 44 Cf. my article on *The Sleep of the Soul in early Syriac Church* in the JAOS, April, 1920, pp. 103—120, and *Monatsschrift f. Gesch. u. Wissensch. d. Judenth.*, 1899, pp. 64 ff.

[5] In *Pat. Syr.*, pars I, col I, s. v. *Aphraates' Doctrina-praefatio*, pp. xlix-xl. That Aph. calls Pharaoh Necho, "Pharaoh the Lame" (ܠܡܐ ܦܪܥܘܢ 972 : 6—7) does not involve any individual indebtedness to Jewish tradition since it had already thus interpreted the text in the Peshitto.

[6] *E. g.*, 268 : 18—19.

to Deuteronomy (ed. Friedmann, sec. 27) ". . . Only on the day of judgment is recompense dealt out (cf. Hom. VIII, sec. 10), since the soul sleeps till the Great Day. This peculiar conception of a soul slumber . . . was widespread among the Jews in Aphraates' time."[1] It is not to be wondered at that so intimate a connection is discerned between Aphraates and Judaism,[2] if it be recalled that in language, geographical proximity, and in respect to a kind of imputed spiritual ancestry, he was at one with them. Furthermore the distinction suggested above, between apologetic and dogmatic, had no need to be drawn. There was a common appeal to a common authority—the Law and its traditional interpretation.

Concrete instances of Aphraates' dependence upon Jewish thought, and affiliation with it.

1. Aphraates' doctrine of (a) Creation, man, and the soul.

Aphraates' references to the Creation follow the text of Genesis, but much of what he says embodies elements of an undoubtedly Jewish origin. In Hom. XVII, commenting on Psalm 90[1, 2] he says: "Know, beloved, that all creatures above and below were first created, then after them all, man. For when God first considered creating the world and all its adornments, from the very first He conceived and shaped man in His Mind. After He had conceived man in His thought, He then conceived the creatures. . . . In conception man is, therefore, older than the creatures, and previous to them. In birth they are older than man and previous to him . . . . . When God had completed the world and adorned it so that there was nothing lacking to it, then He begat Adam from His mind. He molded man with His own hands . . . . and God placed him over all His works, as a man who wishes to make a marriage feast for his son, procures a wife for him, builds

---

[1] S. v. "Aphraates", by Louis Ginzberg, J. E., vol. I, pp. 663—664.

[2] In a very interesting article, *Eine synagogale Parallele zu den B*[e]*nai Q'jâmâ*, Gerh. Kittel observes: *Interessant genug bleibt es für die Zusammenhänge von Synagoge und Kirche, dass mindestens der Name einer christlichen Organisations-form von der ersteren übernommen wurde*, (ZNTW, 1915, vol. XVI, pp. 235—236). Cf. M. Grünwald, *Über das Verhältniss der Kirchenväter zur talmudisch-midraschischen Literatur*, 1891; M. Friedländer, *Patristische und talmudische Studien*, Vienna, 1878.

the house, and provides everything his son may need ... Thus
after He had conceived Adam, God begat him and gave Him
rule over every creature."[1] Of the several unbiblical elements in
this account, counterparts exist in contemporaneous Jewish literature. There is a distinction drawn, for example, between the six
things which preceded the creation of the creatures. "Some of
these were (actually) created and others God had in His mind
to create ... The Torah and the Throne of Glory were created....
The Fathers, Israel, the Holy Sanctuary, and the Name of the
Messiah arose in the mind of the Creator."[2] "The Spirit hovering
over the face of the waters", according to R. Simeon ben Lakish,
was the "soul of the King Messiah",[3] which thus evidently must
have preexisted creation. The words of Ps. 139[5] were taken to
refer to the creation of man. Thus, R. Jochanan couples them
with Gen. 1[26], and Rabbi Akiba says that "after" (אחור) refers to
the first day, and "before" (קדם), to the last day (of creation).
He applies the words of Gen. 1[24] to the soul of Adam. R. Simeon
b. Lakish, on the other hand, says: "'After', (that is, after) the
work of the last day, and "before" the work of the first day".[4]
There seems to be a faint hint at the thought afterward developed
by Aphraates in these words of R. Simeon.

Again, according to a Jewish tradition "Adam was created on
Sabbath eve .... that he might at once go to a meal. It is like
a human king who has built a palace, and when he has it completed then spreads a feast, and afterwards invites the guests".[5] Thus
Adam was created last in order that all things might be ready
for him.[6] That God distinguished man from the rest of His
Creation by molding him with His own hands, while the creatures
were made by the word of His mouth is frequently alluded to.[7]
Adam had two conspicuous advantages over creaturedom: he

[1] 797 : 1—3; 3—10; 11—15; 17—19.
[2] Mid. Ber. Rab. 1 5.
[3] Ibid., 8[a].
[4] Ibid.
[5] Sanh. 38[a], cf. parallel in St. James of Edessa (who may be indebted also to
Aph.) in L. Ginzberg, Die Haggada bei den Kirchenvätern, p. 24.
[6] Tosefta Sanh. 8 7-9 upon which follows the above quotation of Sanh. 38[a].
[7] E. g., in the "Alphabet Midrash" of R. Akiba, (ed. Jellinek, col. 3, p. 59).

was made by the very hands of God, and was also the culmination of the process of creation. "Each successive thing in creation bears the rule over that which was created before it: thus the firmament over the heavens, the herb over the firmament, ... and (God said to man) ye are created after all to have the rule over all".[1] The serpent tempted Eve by urging her to eat of the fruit of the tree "lest other worlds be created, and they rule over you", and thus man might forfeit the preeminence he now held.[2] We may see from these examples how Aphraates combines several Jewish elements in the piecing together of his first creation story in the seventeenth homily. Even a superficial examination shows that its tenor and method are obviously quite in the style of the Rabbis.

Aphraates further says of the original endowment of Adam, that "after God begat man from His thought, and molded him and breathed His Spirit into him, He gave him the power of discrimination, of knowing good from evil, and the power of acknowledging His Creator as his Maker".[3] This "breathing into man of His Spirit" is what Aphraates in another place calls the natural soul (ܢܦܫܐ ܟܝܢܝܬܐ), and it was given at the "first birth" (ܡܘܠܕܐ ܩܕܡܝܐ). This is created in man, and is immortal.[4] The Pauline doctrine of "natural" and "spiritual" (cf. I Cor. 15) is of course back of his thought when he says: "At the day of Resurrection, those who have not been changed will remain in their natural state in the nature of the earth which Adam had, and will abide on the earth below".[5] Even in this case, the "natural" soul is conceived of as being immortal, though it is of a different quality of immortality to the "spiritual" soul given by Baptism. What I wish to suggest here is that Aphraates was convinced of the immortal character of the life principle with which Adam—

[1] Thus R. Jehuda bar Simon, in *Mid. Ber. Rab.* 19ᵇ.

[2] R. Joshua in the name of R. Levi, *ibid*.

[3] 800 : 2—6.

[4] 293 : 5—9. Aphraates believed in a second birth, and a special gift of the Spirit through Baptism,—by compensation, through the work of Jesus, for the presence of the Spirit lost through sin, but this topic need not be entered upon here.

[5] 309 : 11—13.

and his descendants—were endowed, and to note that the gift of
this immortal principle carried with it (a) the capacity for
speech, and (b) the faculty for the recognition of God as man's
Lord and Creator.

The Targum Onkelos on Gen. 2 [7] translates נפש חיה by רוחא
ממללא thus implying the association between the power of speech
and the gift of the "living soul". According to Aphraates when
man recognized and acknowledged his Creator, then God took
up His dwelling in man, "being formed and conceived in the
mind of man, who (thereby) became the Temple of God".[1] On
the other hand, failure thus to acknowledge God reduces the
deniers to the level of the animals, and such men "were accounted
as beasts before Him".[2] Aphraates is perfectly certain that the
presence of God in the individual is determined by the free will
of man, who can either accept or reject his proper allegiance.[3]
According to the Jewish tradition Adam, after naming the animals,
being asked by God who He was, answered: "Thy Name is
Adonai, for Thou art the Lord of all Thy Creation."[4] R. bar
Chama said that when Adam refused to recognize His Creator
he "became as a beast".[5]

b) The Fall, death, and the curse.

Aphraates believed that there was a loss of this presence of
God at the Fall. Man's sin brought the curse of death upon Adam
and his posterity.[6] His sin was disobedience, and the curse pro-
nounced upon him was the penalty of labor, because of the curse
upon the earth for Adam's sake, and death. God gave Adam
an opportunity to repent: "When Adam had sinned, God called
him to repentance, when He said: 'Adam, where art thou?' But
he concealed his sin from the Searcher of hearts, and brought

---

[1] 800 : 6—9.

[2] Ps. 73 [32] : 800 : 15—16.

[3] Aph. even distinguished a service of God undertaken freely and without
command, a "work of supererogation"—as it were, cf. 845 : 19—25.

[4] *Mid. Ber. Rab.* 17 5.

[5] In *Sanh.* 38[a], and cf. *Pesikta R.* 34[a] (at end).

[6] 324 : 6—11; 992 : 6—19 (cf. Rom. 5 [12], [14]); II : 9 : 5—13, etc.

accusation against Eve that she had deceived him. For the
reason that he had not acknowledged his sin, (God) decreed
upon him death, and (also) upon all his posterity".[1] "On the day
thou eatest of it *thou shalt surely die*" is interpreted in the Targum
Jonathan: "thou shalt become worthy of death".[2] Aphraates says:
"When God laid the injunction upon Adam ... and afterwards
Adam transgressed it, and ate, he lived nine hundred and thirty
years, but because of his sin he was as dead before God".[3]

Part of the first quotation of Aphraates is almost word for
word given in the *Midrash R.* to Numbers. "R. Tanchuma b. Aba
said ... when Adam had transgressed the command of the Holy
One .... and had eaten of the tree, the Holy One looked for
him to make an act of repentance, but he did not".[4] The words
מות תמות are taken to imply the curse of death on Adam's
descendants, as well as on himself and Eve.[5] God said of man:
"If he sin, he shall die, and if he sin not, he shall live".[6] Death
followed man's sin, but Adam did not die immediately: "When I
said, 'On the day thou eatest of it thou shalt surely die', ye knew
not whether I meant one of my days, or one of yours. 'Behold
I give one of my days of a thousand years', and Adam lived
nine hundred and thirty years, and left the seventy years to his
sons".[7] (While Adam lost the term of his natural life, still God
gave him life for one of His own days,—cf. Ps. 90[4]). Aphraates
said that Adam was "dead" because he was in sin, and speaks
of those who, while still alive in the flesh, are really dead spiritually
because of their sins.[8] The lot of the righteous on whom the
curse even of death rested in spite of their holiness, was a subject
for rabbinical disputation. God answered the angels, who asked
Him why Adam had died, by saying: "Because he did not carry

---

[1] 324 : 6—11.

[2] מות חיב תהי for מות תמות of Gen. 2 [17].

[3] 393 : 2—7; cf. also Hom. XXIII, sec. 14, etc.

[4] 13 5. (*Mid. Rab. Ber.*)

[5] *Mid. Rab. Ber.* 16 [10].

[6] *Ibid.* 8 [11].

[7] Cf. Ps. 90[10]—*Mid. R. Ber.* 19[14]. On this cf. Parisot's introduction pp. lviii—lix,
and Ginzberg, *Die Haggada bei den Kirchenvätern.* pp. 48—49.

[8] 393 21—23.

out my command".[1] Yet Moses and the great patriarchs had
died, and Moses had not committed sin as had Adam. When
Moses thus appealed to God, God yet decreed death upon him;
"because of the sin of the First Man thou art to die, for he
brought death into the world".[2] R. Levi illustrated this same
doctrine by the parable of the child born during his mother's
imprisonment. "When he grew up it chanced that one day the
King passed by the prison, and the youth appealed: 'Why, my
Lord King, am I bound in prison?' The King answered: 'This
is due to thy mother's sin'".[3] "There is one event to the righteous
and to the wicked man, to the good and to the pure".[4] R. Ami
said: "There is no death without sin . . . . . Upon Adam was
decreed death because he transgressed a very light command of
God . . . . Why then did Moses and Aaron die? Because there
is one event", etc.[5] The application of the text quoted to Moses
and Aaron is made in the *Mid. Koheleth, ad loc.*[6]

One Jewish tradition finds the same solution of the difficulty
regarding the relative lots of the evil and good on earth, that
death reigns over both alike, as is suggested by Aphraates.[7] In
commenting on the text of Eccl. 9[5] a *midrash* is given to the
effect that "the living know that they will die,—this refers to the
righteous who are called 'living' even though they die; the dead
have no knowledge—this means the wicked, who though living
are called 'dead'. Thus in the text 'about the land which I
sware unto Abraham, Isaac and Jacob, saying, etc.'[8] God spake
not to the Fathers,—Abraham, Isaac and Jacob,—but to Moses:
'Go, and say to them that I have fulfilled my oath which I sware
to them', saying 'to thy seed shall I give it'. But the wicked are
called 'dead', as it is said, (Ezek. 11) . . . This refers to the wicked
who in their lifetime are called 'dead'."[9] But Aphraates meant
more by his use of the thought than that the wicked are "called

---

[1] *Sifre* 141[a].   [2] *Mid R. Debarim* 9[4]
[3] *Ibid.*   [4] Eccl. 9[2].   [5] *Sab.* 55[b].
[6] 9[1]: Moses is "the good". Cf. Ex. 2[2], and Aaron "the pure" since he is
concerned with the laws of purification.
[7] For a quite different one, cf. *Mid. Ber. R.* 9[7].
[8] Numbers 32[11].
[9] *Mid. Koheleth* 9[4].

dead". He understood that on their higher spiritual side they were actually without the indwelling Spirit of God. The wicked forfeit the Spirit's presence as he does who refuses to recognize and acknowledge His Creator—and are thereby reduced to the level of animals, saving only that they are immortal.

As we have seen, Aphraates believed that repentance on Adam's part would have restored him to God's favor. "The folly of Adam consisted in not saying 'I have sinned' but in maintaining his innocence."[1] The contrast to "folly" is "wisdom", the end of which is repentance and good works.[2] "Happy is he who sins not, and if he sin, repent, that it be well with him."[3] According to R. Simeon b. Lakish, Adam was not driven from the Garden of Eden until he had reviled and blasphemed God.[4] Adam's sin lost him his place in the Garden, and he incurred the double curse of labor and death.

The curse laid upon the serpent is related by Aphraates as follows: "When the serpent was jealous of Adam in paradise he incurred upon himself a threefold curse: God deprived him of his feet, and he crawled upon his belly; he took away his food, and gave him dust (for food); he made him the enemy whom man should tread under foot,[5]—since on his feet he had come to commit sin, and had attacked Adam, and through food had seduced Eve."[6] So the serpent gained a certain power over mankind by the Fall, for "we are the food of the serpent."[7] The fact that dust was to be the serpent's food (Gen. 3 [14]) and was also that to which man, by the curse laid upon him, "was to return" (Gen. 3 [20]) establishes the inference which Aphraates drew that man was the food ܡܐܟܘܠܬܐ of the serpent.[8]

According to Jewish tradition, God was willing to treat with Adam and Eve and would have forgiven them on their showing

---

[1] Quoted from *Mid. Ber. R.* by Funk, *op. cit.*, pp. 20—21.
[2] For parallels cf. Hershon, *Homesh .... lephi Hattalmud*, p. 141, etc.
[3] *Suc.* 53[a].
[4] *Mid. Ber. R.* 1922.
[5] 424 : 25—26; 425 : 1—4.
[6] 600 : 1—5.
[7] 89 : 19—20.
[8] 676 : 20—21; 732 : 18—19; 241 : 2—3; 6—7, etc.

signs of repentance, but He refused to deal with the serpent,—
"an evil beast and a master at repartee."[1] "As the First Man
sat in the Garden and the ministering angels roasted flesh and
chilled wine for him, the serpent taking note of these attentions,
and observing his happy state, grew jealous,"[2] and then plotted
his downfall. He was also jealous of Adam and wanted Eve for
himself.[3] "When the Holy One . . . said to the serpent, 'upon thy
belly shalt thou go,' the ministering angels descended and cut
off his hands and feet, and his cry was heard from one end of
the world to the other . . . . ."[4] R. Asi and R. Hoshaia explain it
thus: ". . . .God said 'I made thee King over cattle and animals,
and thou didst not seek it; I made thee to walk upright like a
man, and thou didst not seek it;—'upon thy belly shalt thou go';
I made thee to eat food like a man, but thou didst not desire
it,—and 'dust thou shall eat all the days of thy life'; thou didst
desire to slay Adam and to take Eve to thyself,—and 'I have
set enmity between thee and the woman . . .' "[5]

The sin on Adam's part,—according to Aphraates—was his
pride.[6] "Because (through pride) he hearkened to the serpent
the first man received as penalty that he should become his food."[7]
Eve's fall was occasioned by her weakness in yielding to temptation, and the appeal, in her case, was to the flesh.[8] Thus the
fall in Jewish tradition is attributed to Adam's pride and disobedience, to Eve's lust, to the wiles of the serpent, and to the
deceit of Satan.[9] Aphraates says in homily XII that the serpent
was none other than Satan.[10] The Devil foiled God's plan for
raising man even to a still higher state, should he have obeyed

---

[1] *Mid. Ber. R.* 20 3.

[2] *Sanh.* 59ᵇ; cf. Aph. 424 : 25—26; 425 : 1—4.

[3] *Mid. Ber. R.* 20 11.

[4] *Mid. Ber. R.* 20 8.

[5] *Ibid,* 20 11. Lust was the chief reason for the serpent's deed, according to
Sota 9ᵃ⁻ᵇ, where substantially the same account is repeated with a slightly different
coloring.

[6] 592 : 16—18; 591 : 15—16; 439 : 25—26.

[7] II : 5 : 9—12.

[8] Cf. Hom. XXIII, especially sec. 3.

[9] Cf. *Sifrê,* § שלש; *Mid. Ber. R.* 19 8.

[10] 524 : 17—18.

God's command.[1] In the last resort, R. Simeon B. Lakish says all evil is traceable to a single source, for "Satan, the evil *yeṣer*, and the angel of Death are all one."[2]

2. (a) Sin and the *yeṣer hara*.

It is because of his evil *yeṣer* ("impulse"), according to the Rabbis, that a man sins. Man has properties in common with the animals below, and also qualities that are from above. Of the six works of creation, some were from above, and some from below. When it came time to create man, God said: "'If I create him from that which is above, then such works will outnumber those from below, and if I create him from that which is below, they will outnumber the former . . . . I shall create him from that which is both above and below, as it is written, 'and God the Lord moulded Adam,'[3] etc.,—of dust from the earth,—from below,—and breathed into his nostrils the breath of life,—from above'."[4] The doctrine of the two *yeṣers* was attached to the text Gen. 2 7, in which the word וייצר has two yods,—"this means the good *yeṣer* and the evil *yeṣer*."[5] The word itself might mean (a) something which God has made, or (b) something which man works,[6] according to F. C. Porter.[7] The rabbis dealt with the practical method to escape sin and conquer it, rather than with any speculations regarding its origin. They were following the line of the teaching of the apocryphal and pseudepigraphical literature in so doing.[8] The sequence in history is noted, but it is regarded as rather a temporal than a causal

---

[1] 439 : 16—25.

[2] *Baba Bathra* 97 ᵃ.

[3] Gen. 2 7.

[4] *Mid. Rab. Ber.* 12 7.

[5] *Ibid.,* 14 4.

[6] Cf. Deut. 31 ²¹.

[7] *The Yeçer Hara,* in *Yale Biblical and Semitic Studies,* pp. 91—156; reference above *ibid.,* p, 108—109.

[8] Cf. Wisdom 2 ²³ ff.; Ecclus. 25 ²⁴; IV Ezra 37: "Mandasti Adam deligere viam tuam et praeterivit; et statim instituisti in eum mortis et in nationibus (generationibus) ejus"; "Adam mortem intulit"—Apoc. Bar. 17 ³; cf. *ibid.* 23 4; "Non est Adam causa nisi animae suae", *ibid.* 54 ¹⁵, ¹⁹.

sequence. It is in line with the Semitic way of thinking to conceive of events in a *temporal* sequence, while the Greek mind would be prone to find rather a *causal* sequence in the same facts. The theologians who followed the speculative philosophers of Greece found in Adam's sin the cause of our own sinning. Hence was developed the theory of "original sin." The Rabbis were not concerned with the speculative problems. "Original sin" is not a rabbinic doctrine.[1] The "Fall of man .... can mean .... only the original experience of the individual .... It cannot refer to mankind as a whole, for the human race has never experienced a fall, nor is it affected by original or hereditary sin."[2] The question in the rabbinic mind was rather how to deal with the ever present problem, than to speculate about its origin.

The doctrine of the *'yeṣer hattob'* and the *'yeṣer hara'* is the rabbinic method of meeting the problem. The evil impulse and the good impulse were both created in man by God.[3] "It does not appear that its origin was traced to man's sin. It must have explained his sin."[4] The philosophical difficulty involving an inherently evil disposition in man as God made him, is not grappled with by the Rabbis.[5] The Rabbis speculated when it was given man, whether at birth or before,[6] but in any case they conclude that the evil impulse does not make itself felt until a certain age has been reached. "God made man that he should become righteous. If you ask, 'how is it possible for one to make good what God has made evil?'[7] God answers, 'thou hast made it to be evil.' A babe sins not, nor a five, six, seven, eight or nine year-old child, but at ten and from then on the evil impulse grows, and the Holy One says: 'Thou hast made it evil.'[8] The soul comes pure from the hands of God and must be returned

---

[1] I. Lévi, *Le péché originel*, Paris, 1909. (2nd Ed.); Edersheim, *Life and Times of Jesus the Messiah*, I. ·p. 165.

[2] K. Kohler, *Jewish Theology*, N. Y. 1908, p. 225.

[3] Cf. treatment of the question in *Yoma* 69 b.

[4] F. C. Porter, *The Yeçer Hara*, p. 108.

[5] *Ibid*, p. 117.

[6] *Mid. Ber. R.* 34 12.

[7] Cf. Gen. 8 21 b.

[8] *Mid. Tanchuma Ber*. 7; also cf. *Mid. Koheleth Rab.* 4 15.

to Him in purity."[1] Consequently each man sins of himself;
Adam was the cause of his own, and no one's else sin.[2]

Some of the other Rabbinic passages have been interpreted to
involve a real dualism between spirit and matter. Thus Weber[3]
says that the evil *yeṣer* inheres in pre-existent matter, which
always manifests a certain character of rebellion against God.
He adds that it is resident in the material part of man, while
the good *yeṣer* inheres in his spiritual faculties. That Weber is
quite wrong is shown conclusively by Porter.[4] For example,
Weber's translation of גוף as "body" is misleading, as is clear
from such a passage as *Aboth* 4[10]: "whosoever honors the law is
himself (מכובד) honored." There is no dualism in Rabbinic theology.
Man is considered a unity of body and soul,[5] and both are
essential to the notion of *man*. There is no opposition between
matter and spirit discernible in Judaism. "The Greek idea of the
material body as the seat and source of sin gained difficult and
limited access to the Jewish mind".[6] "The Rabbis are never
dualists after Plato's kind. It is man that sins, and man is neither
body nor soul, but the union of the two."[7]

The evil and the good *yeṣer* both reside in the moral person,
the inner self. They inhere in the same body and soul. "The
heart of wisdom on the right hand,[8] that is, the good impulse ....
the heart of folly on the left, that is, the evil impulse."[9] The evil
yeṣer is conceived of not only as a resident passion or impulse
but even as a foreign and alien element. While it is in man, it
is not of him, as in the highest stratum of man's constitution.
R. Jochanan b. Nuri said: "This is the way the evil *yeṣer* operates:
to-day it may say to a man, 'do this' (to-morrow, 'do that') and

---

1 *Mid. Koheleth Rabbati* 12 7.

2 As in *Apoc. Bar.* 54 15, 19.

3 *Jüdische Theologie*, pp. 201 ff.

4 *Op. cit.*, pp. 104—106, etc.

5 M. Lazarus, *Die Ethik des Judentums*, Frankfurt a. M., 1898 p. 268.

6 Porter, *op. cit.* p. 145, cf. also pp 153—156; also Lazarus, *op. cit.*, p. 267.

7 F. C. Porter, *The Preexistence of the Soul in the Book of Wisdom, and in the Rabbinic Writings*, A. J. T. vol. 12 (1908) no. 1, p. 103; cf. p. 96.

8 Cf. Eccl. 10 2.

9 *Mid. Bamidbar R.* 27 8.

finally it tells him to commit idolatry and he does ... R. Abin
said: 'from what text is this derived? (from the words)[1] 'there
shall not be in thee any strange God, thou shalt not worship
any alien Divinity.' What sort is this 'strange God?' It is the
evil *yeṣer*."[2] The evil *yeṣer* has led astray whole peoples.[3] Occasion-
ally it is conceived of as an almost personal alien power: "The
evil *yeṣer* misleads men in this world, and in the world to come
acts as διάβολος against them".[4] Raba says that it is at first
called the "traveler", the "guest", and then after sojourning a time
in man takes up its permanent abode in him, and acts as master.[5]

It is an overwhelming outside force, a passion. Bacher interprets the controversy between R. Akiba and R. Meir about the
evil *yeṣer* by saying that the point of their conclusions is that
the greatest moral strength without divine protection is not
sufficient to protect a man against its onslaughts.[6] Only the
special help of God given in answer to prayer avails to make
man's struggle against the evil impulse victorious.[7] "God decrees
all the events of man's life, but whether he be righteous or
wicked, He does not predetermine, but this matter is left in man's
own hand(s), as it is said: 'behold I have put before thee to-day
life, the good, death, and the evil'."[8] The great moral struggle
is to give the allegiance of the will and deed to the rightful
lord. The evil *yeṣer* is likened to a foolish old king, the good
yeṣer to a young but poor king. The force of the comparison
lies in the fact that the latter does not receive the full allegiance
of all men, and is therefore "poor", but yet wise, "since the good
yeṣer incites to wise actions and the way of righteousness".[9]
They only who obey the behests of the good *yeṣer* can be said
really to possess life.[10]

---

[1] Psalm 81 9.   [2] *Sabbath* 105[h].
[3] *Mid. Koheleth R.* 4 [16].
[4] *Suc.* 52[b]; cf. below, that God will publicly slay the evil *yeṣer*, etc.
[5] *Suc.* 52[b], [a].
[6] *Die Agada der Tannaiten*, vol. I, p. 284.
[7] For discussion, cf. Porter, *The Yeçer Hara*, pp. 123 ff.
[8] *Mid. Tanchuma, Pikude* 4.
[9] Cf. *Mid. Koheleth R.* 4 [15].
[10] *Mid. Koheleth R.* 4 [16].

In the majority of men the evil *yeṣer* is the stronger, and the good *yeṣer* the weaker.[1] The great moral struggle is to dethrone the evil *yeṣer* and set up the rightful king. "All the time the righteous live, they do battle with their (evil) impulse."[2] He must so fight that source of sin which is in him, and yet is not identical with him. Man did not transgress the command laid on him save by the interior struggling[3] and victory of this unclean spirit. As the impulse of this alien, but yet resident, power, is always to evil, *yeṣer* alone usually has the connotation of the "evil *yeṣer*". According to Porter, "it frequently stands unmodified and always . . . . in the evil sense."[4] The Rabbis usually employ it with its bad connotation. The Rabbinic use is in evidence in most of Ben Sirach,[5] in the *granum seminis mali* of 2 Esdras, and in *Apoc. Baruch*. The appearance of the Rabbinic use dates from the 2ⁿᵈ cent. B. C.[6] The deduction from Biblical texts, such as Gen. 8²¹, was not out of accord with general Rabbinic conclusions that "that leaven is truly unfortunate whose baker witnesses of it that 'it is evil from its youth.'"[7] When the word is used without attributive or predicate adjective it is understood to mean the evil impulse.[8]

God only can give the grace necessary to conquer it in this life,[9] and He will publicly slay the evil *yeṣer* at the last day.[10] God's might is necessary in this life to hold its power in check, and at the best to enable the individual not to be conquered by it. God will finally reveal it, slay it in the world to come, and forever destroy its power over men. Meanwhile the struggle goes on in this world. "Blessed is he that considereth the poor

---

[1] *Nedarim* 32ᵇ.   [2] *Mid. Ber. R.* 9⁷.

[3] *Sota* 3ᵃ.

[4] *Op. cit.*, p. 109.

[5] Except perhaps in 15¹⁴, and 21¹¹ᵃ (?).

[6] Cf. Levy, *Wörterbuch*: Jastrow's Dictionary s. v. יצר for confirmation of this use.

[7] *Mid. Ber. R.* 34¹².

[8] S. Schechter, *Some Aspects of Rabbinic Judaism*, pp. 242—92, esp. p. 362. F. C. Porter, *The Yeṣer Hara*, pp. 106—9; M. Lazarus, *Die Ethik des Judentums*, pp. 263—8.

[9] Cf. *Succa* 52ᵃ.

[10] R. Jehuda said: "In the world to come the Holy One . . . will bring forth the evil impulse, (יצר) and slay it before both the righteous and the wicked." *Succa* 52ᵇ.

and needy: the Lord will deliver him in the time of trouble"[1] according to Abba bar Yarmiah, speaking in the name of R. Meir, "is he who caused the good *yeṣer* to rule (שׁהמׁליׁך) over the evil *yeṣer*".[2] Proverbs 24 [21] is another text which has reference to "king", 'he who should rule over him',—this means the good *yeṣer* who is to rule over the evil *yeṣer*.[3]

b) "Original Sin"; Jewish teaching and Aphraates.

In Aphraates we find no doctrine of original sin. If St. Paul in his Epistle to the Romans was thinking as a Greek and not as a Jew, then Aphraates has surely failed to grasp his meaning.[4] Adam sinned, and all of his descendants as well, save only the "One innocent among all the children of men." The sequence from Adam's sin to that of his offspring was temporal, not causal. It is clear from what is shown above, that Aphraates believed Adam's sin to have been the result of his own choice and pride, whereby he followed the temptation suggested by the Evil One and disobeyed God. While he does not say that his evil *yeṣer* caused Adam to sin, his view of sin is entirely consonant otherwise with Rabbinic thought. The Rabbis did not trace sin to Adam's Fall, but rather explained his sin by the doctrine of the evil *yeṣer*. In Aphraates there is no dualism between spirit and matter. There is an opposition, which he shares with Judaism, between good and evil, but there is not the faintest connection between "evil" and matter as such, or "good" and spirit at such. Again he shares the Rabbinic point of view. A still stronger resemblance is found in Aphraates' conviction,—so utterly taken for granted that it not only not defended or questioned, but not even explicitly stated,—that man is a unity. "Man" consists of the union of body and soul. A clear corollary from this principle

---

[1] Ps. 41 1.   [2] *Mid. Vayyikra R.* 34 1.

[3] *Mid. Tanchuma Behaalothecha* 2.

[4] *E. g.*, on Rom. 5 19 cf. Bethune-Baker, *History of Christian Doctrine*, p. 17; *St. P.* may have had the "cor malignun" of Bar 1 22, and 2 Esd. 3 25 ("deliquerunt . . . facientes sicut Adam et omnes generationes ejus") in mind; Sanday and Headlam, *ad loc.*: "something else at work besides the guilt of individuals . . . the effect of Adam's fall" (*Commentary* p. 134). S. & H. reject the idea of a dualism in St. P.; *vide op. cit.*, pp. 174, 181.

can be seen in the doctrine of the "sleep of the soul." The soul
of the believer is buried in the earth with his body, and there
will sleep[1] till the Day of Resurrection. The Spirit given at
Baptism has returned at the believer's death to heaven. At the
Resurrection the "Spirit" will return to its tenement, and body,
soul, and spirit are again united, and the whole man stands
before God for judgment. So keenly did he feel the implication
of this eminently Jewish conception that he could not think of
the punishing or rewarding of the body apart from the soul.

Again, Aphraates always uses[2] ܝ in the normal Rabbinic
sense, when undefined, as the evil *yeṣer*, following the meaning
of the word in such passages as Gen. 6 5, 8 21, Deut. 31 21. The
equivalent of the יצר הטוב is to be found, I believe, in combination
with another eminently Jewish conception,—in Aphraates' doctrine
of the indwelling Holy Spirit. As was said above, Aphraates
taught that God was born in man when he by a free act of will
acknowledged and recognized His Creator. This indwelling
presence of God in the heart of man, His creature, is lost by
sin. Aphraates intimates that the sinner loses the presence of
God by his sin, in that sin, (disobediance), is a declaration of
unbelief or a repudiation of God's primary relation to man as
Creator and Lord. The text of Gen. 6 3 in the *Peshitto* reads:
ܠܐܠܡ ܠܐܠܡ ܪܘܚ ܗܘܐ. ܕܠܐ ܕܘ܃, and while Aphraates never explicitly
quotes it, I believe that in it lies the key to his doctrine of Sin,
the Fall, and Redemption. If the effect of sin be the loss of
God's Spirit, lost to each man by his own free will, and pre-
eminently in the case of the typical Man, Adam, redemption is
the restoration of that Spirit to mankind. As a matter of fact,
this is precisely Aphraates' doctrine of Redemption: the importation
into sinful humanity of the Spirit through the work and life of
Jesus, by which all the consequences of the Fall were obliterated,
and mankind raised to the position which God had predestined
for it. The means of the 'injection', so to speak, of this lost

---

[1] Cf. my article on the *Sleep of the Soul* in JAOS, April, 1920, pp. 103—120.

[2] Cf. 100 : 1—2; 416 : 17—18; 605 : 1, etc.

[3] Hebrew לא ידון; LXX has καταμείνῃ,—the probable Heb. reading back of
the LXX was: לא ידור or לא ילון.

principle into mankind, was the Incarnation. The fruits of the Incarnation were made available to believers through the Sacraments. The Spirit was in the waters of Baptism, and by the performance of the rite it entered the believer.

"The King", and the "King's Son", to Aphraates, is the "Spirit" or "Spirit of Christ".[1] "It is not fitting ... that from the portal by which entered the King should go forth refuse and filth;[2] ... the mouth through which entered the Son of the King should be carefull guarded".[3] "Let us magnify the King's son who is with us ... he who receives the King's Son with honour has many gifts given him by the King .... What may we do in our poverty for the King's Son?"[4] "The dedicated virgin is espoused to the King, to whom she gives allegiance and service".[5] The proper rules for the entertainment of this "humble anointed King"[6] whom unbelievers and sinners reject, are the precepts of the spiritual life. As this "Spirit" (of Christ) is primarily the Spirit of life, so Death is conceived of as the Spirit of evil. As in the case of the evil $yeṣer$, destruction of death is the work of God,— but in Aphraates it is to be through Christ.[7] The gift of immortality is pledged now, and is to be realized hereafter in the world to come.

According to Jewish tradition "the generation of the Flood shall have no portion in the world to come, nor shall they stand in the judgment" ... (then, quoting Gen. 6[3]), "for theirs is no "judgment" and no "Spirit".[8] A closer parallel to some of the elements of Aphraates' thought is traceable in the Rabbinic doctrine of the Shechina. "When Adam sinned the Shechina was withdrawn to the first heaven; Cain sinned and it was withdrawn to the second heaven; at the time of the generation of Enosh it was withdrawn to the third heaven,"[9] etc. By prayer, acts of virtue, and the merits of the great Patriarchs, it is restored to proximity to man, etc. Sufficient has been suggested to show

---

[1] 101 : 20—25.

[2] Alluding to the Eucharist, by which the Spirit of Christ entered the believer.

[3] 280 : 14.   [4] 280 : 16—17, 20—21.

[5] 272 : 5—6.   [6] 428 : 14.   [7] Cf. homily XXIII, sec. 4.

[8] *Sanhedrin* 107[b].   [9] *Mid. Bammidbar* 13 4.

where Aphraates obtained the elements he pieced into the frame-
work of his Christian theology, which was simply the N. T.
interpreted from the standpoint of the "Asianic School," seen
through the eyes of the Semite.

3. Eschatology and chiliasm.

A brief notice of Aphraates' affiliations in respect to eschatology
and chiliasm will serve as a close to this section. Aphraates
justifies the Resurrection in exactly the same way as does, e. g.,
R. Gebiha b. Pesisa.[1] "If those who have not yet lived can come
into existence, how much more shall they live (again) who have
already died."[2] His argument is of the same familiar type, the
קל וחמר, so frequently employed by the Rabbis. Of the general
type of Aphraates' eschatology it may be said that it was in
part influenced by such a point of view as that of Josephus:
"Our bodies are mortal and made of perishable matter, but part
of the Godhead, an immortal soul, dwells in mortal bodies."[3]
The Philonic doctrine of Josephus is rather more akin to Aphraates' thought than that of the Rabbis who, while they recognized
the Divine principle in the soul, did not regard it as a "part of
the Godhead," but rather viewed it as like the other creatures,—
bearing the *likeness* of their Creator.[4] "This world is the anteroom
in which prepare thyself that thou mayest be able to enter into
the palace."[6] Hence the duty of preparation for the life to come
is incumbent upon all. R. Pinchas ben Yair saw that the means
of making ready for the future life consisted in "obedience to the
law, hence . . . . . purity, humility, sinlessness, sanctity, possession
of the Holy Spirit, and immortality."[7] The various texts used in
proving from the Torah the doctrine of the immortality of the
soul are those which Aphraates himself uses,—Deut. 22 7,[8]

---

[1] *Sank.* 91 [2].   [2] 369 : 19—23.

[3] *De bello Jud.* III. 8. 5.

[4] Aug. Wünsche, *Die Vorstellungen vom Zustande nach dem Tode nach Apocrypha,
Talmud und Kirchenvätern, J. P. T.* (vol. 6) 1880, pp. 355—83; 495—523.

[5] *Pirke Aboth* 4 [21].

[6] *Moed Katon* 9 [b].

[7] *Aboda Zara* 20 [b].

[8] *Kid.* 39 [b].

Deut. 31 [16],[1] Deut. 32 [39] [2], Deut. 33 [6] [3], etc. There are few things more definite than the unanimity of conviction among the Rabbis concerning the resurrection of the body. "The soul is without its earthly integument for a time only, and is then to be reunited with it . . . The grave gives back the material composition of the body, which . . . passes in new power to an eternal immortality."[4] The three chief types of argument for the Resurrection are as valid for Aphraates as for the Rabbis. The first type is the "ontological,"[5] and the familiar illustration is derived from a comparison of pottery and blown glass. A blown glass vessel if destroyed can be remade, since it is made by breath (ברוח), while pottery, made by hands, if once smashed is forever incapable of being restored. "Thus with men there is the possibility of rehabilitation, since they are made by the breath of the Holy One" (שברוח של הקב"ה)[6]. The "moral argument," which is the contention of homilies XXI and XXIII of Aphraates, states that without the Resurrection there is no vindication of the righteousness of God, nor compensation for the suffering of the poor and innocent.[7] The "analogical" argument of, for example, R. Tabi in the name of R. Josiah, shows the analogy of the grave to the womb of the pregnant mother.[8] This figure frequently appears in Syriac literature[9] though it does not, so far as I have been able to find, in Aphraates.

An examination of the component elements in Aphraates' doctrine of the "sleep of the soul" will disclose its strong Jewish affiliations. "In the second birth[10] men receive the Holy Spirit, a particle of the Godhead, (ܐ ܒ݁ܪ ܕ݁ܐܠܗܐ) and it will never die. When these men die, the 'soulish' spirit is buried with the body

---

[1] Sanh. 90[b].　　　[2] Pesach. 68[a].

[3] Sanh. 92[a].

[4] Wünsche, op. cit., p. 365.

[5] Cf. Aph. 369 : 19—23; Sanh. 92[a].

[6] Sanhedrin 91[a].

[7] Cf. Pirke Aboth. iv. 29.

[8] Sanh. 92[a]; Berach. 15[b].

[9] Cf. O. Braun, Moses bar Kepha und sein Buch von der Seele, Freiburg i. B., 1891. cf. pp. 145—46; cf. St. Ephraemi Syri Carmina Nisibena . . . ed. G. Bickell, Leipzig, 1866; esp. LXXIII, LXV, LXXI, etc.

[10] I. e., Baptism.

and all sensation is taken from it. The heavenly Spirit which they have received goes back to its nature, to the presence (ܠܘܬ) of Christ. Both these facts the Apostle teaches, for he says: 'The body is buried (ܡܬܩܒܪ) 'soulish' and rises 'spiritual'[2] ... Christ's Spirit which the 'spiritual' (ܪܘܚܢܐ) have received goes back to the Lord's presence: the soulish spirit is buried in its own nature and is deprived of sensation".[3] Just as the servant who awaits punishment on the morrow sleeps uneasily, so does the wicked man awaiting his condemnation; while the righteous sleep well in the grave and have pleasant dreams.[4] The moral capacity is as entirely absent during the sleep of death, as it is in abeyance during natural sleep.[5] The judgment at the last day will be of both soul and body together, since "no one has yet received his reward".[6]

Aside from the very considerable influence of St. Paul in determining the character of Aphraates' eschatology,[7] there is undoubtedly the same conviction at work in Aphraates' thought as in Rabbinic Judaism. "The whole man, body and soul, is judged,"[8] not the soul alone. "The body says, 'the soul has sinned';.. the soul says, 'the body has sinned' .... It is like the case of a man who had a beautiful orchard yielding delicious figs. To guard them .. he put into the orchard two men,—one blind, the other, lame and unable to use his legs. The lame man suggested to the blind man that he carry him on his back, as the only way to get at the figs ... When the master missing his figs, ... accused them, one pleaded: 'thou seest I have no feet

---

1 The *Pesh.* ad loc. has ܙܪܝܥ and the difference between the two verbs "buried" and "sown" has a considerable bearing on Aphraates' doctrine. It is probable that he 'adapted' his text to prove a position taken on other grounds.

2 1. Cor. 15 44: the "soul" (ψυχή) is ܢܦܫ; the "spirit" (πνεῦμα) ܪܘܚ.

3 293:2—24.

4 396:16—5; 397:1—14.

5 397:15—17.

6 401:14—15.

7 Cf. J. St. J. Thackeray, *The Relation of St. Paul to Contemporary Jewish Thought*, Cambridge, 1900. pp. 104—154; Ernst Teichmann, *Die Paulinischen Vorstellungen von Auferstehung und Gericht und ihre Beziehung zur jüdischen Apokalyptik.* Freiburg i. B., 1896, pp. 1—59.

8 Wünsche, *op. cit.,* p. 379.

to bring me to the figs'. The other: 'I have no eyes to see the way to them'. But the master placed the lame man on him who was blind and beat them together".[1] As in Rabbinic Judaism, so in the eschatology of the early Syriac Church, the doctrine of the bodily resurrection was necessary, since: "Der ganze Mensch ist es, der Verdienste oder Missverdienste erwirbt, darum erhält auch der ganze Mensch Lohn oder Strafe".[2]

"The souls of the righteous go directly on high, but those of the ungodly wander about, finding no place to put their feet; . . . their souls go back and forth constantly about the grave for twelve months".[3] This is, however, not the only speculation concerning the state of the souls of the dead. According to some Rabbis, they have no sensations at all,[4] but there are indications that some of the Rabbis believed in much the same doctrine concerning the presence of the soul in the buried body, as did Aphraates. R. Nachman v. Jacob said that "a worm hurts the body of the dead as much as a needle the body of a living person".[5] The departed hear everything spoken of them.[6] Rab asks R. Simeon b. She'ila to deliver a good funeral oration over him that he may enjoy it![7] The judgment will be of all alike, regardless of whether "they be Gentile or Israelite, man or woman, mistress or maid, all will be judged according to deeds, by the Holy Spirit who will pronounce upon them".[8] There will be those wo are "sealed to eternal life" (the righteous), the evil who are "sealed" to hell, and the "middle grade" who have sinned, but repented, and will be punished for a while.[9] Precisely this theory is discernible in Aphraates, for the righteous[10] go immediately to heaven at the last judgment, the wicked to hell, and

---

[1] *Sanhedrin* 91[b].

[2] O. Braun, *Beiträge zur Geschichte der Eschatologie in den Syrischen Kirchen*, Z. K. Th. 1892, vol. XVI. pp. 273—312 (Geo. Patrias p. 280).

[3] *Mid. Tanchuma. Vayyikra*, cf. J. Frey, *Tod, Seelenglaube, und Seelenkult*, Leipzig, 1898; a good summary is found on pp. 228—232, *op. cit.*

[4] *Sab.* 13[b].

[5] *Ber.* 18[b], *Sab.* 13[b], cf. W. Bacher, *Die Agada der Babyl. Am.* p. 80.

[6] *Sab.* 152[b]; *Ber.* 51[b].   [7] *Sanh.* 90[b].

[8] Cf. *Tanna debe Eliyahu*, ed. Friedmann, c. 10. p. 48.

[9] *Rosh Hash.* 16[b]—17[a]; for discussion, cf. Wünsche, *op. cit.*, pp. 380—383; 500—508.

[10] Homily XXIII is in part a theodicy. He calls the righteous "the soul of

the sinners, who have repented, expiate their sins and then go to heaven.

The doctrine of the Spirit in Aphraates shows Jewish affiliations, but yet is not entirely under Jewish influence, inasmuch as the basis of his doctrine is Pauline. Aphraates agrees with the Rabbis, in holding that the Holy Spirit is the immortal principle in man, and the bond between God and man. By implication, at least, the Holy Spirit's loss denotes a forlorn condition of man in Aphraates, from which he can only be rescued by aid from God direct. If the Jewish repudiation of the doctrine of original sin be on the basis that it makes the Presence of the Holy Spirit in every one of no effect,[1] then Aphraates' doctrine may be considered a step forward toward a more clear grasp of the teachings of the Great Church on the subject. If however "the loss of the Spirit" in Aphraates be a combination of the 'Shechinah' doctrine and other Rabbinic speculations on Gen. 6[3] then it is not necessary to see in Aphraates any violent divergence from the broad current of Jewish thought.

The chiliasm of Aphraates is strikingly Jewish. "Our wise teachers have said, in the same way as God assigned six days' time to the (creation of the) world, this six thousand years' time will see its consummation, and then will come the sabbath of God".[2] R. Ketina said that the "world would last six thousand years: two thousand of emptiness, two thousand of the law, and two thousand of the messianic era".[3] It was a belief which was widespread in Rabbinic Judaism that Aphraates reflects in the quotation above.[4] This Rabbinic speculation came into the Church, and is especially noticeable in Papias, as quoted by Eusebius

the world". Cf. "The righteous an everlasting foundation" (*Yoma* 38[b]) and Aphraates 18 : 13; and Rabba b. b. Chana in *Sanh.* 103[a].

[1] Cf. H. Cohen, *Der Heilige Geist* in *Festschrift zum 70 ten Geburtstag J. Guttmans*, Leipsig, 1915, pp. 1—21 ... "Die Erbsünde ist unmöglich, ihr Gedanke überwunden, (weil) sie widerspricht dem heiligen Geiste, der dem Menschen mit Gott gemeinsam ist". (P. 15. *ibid.*)

[2] 77 : 8—13, on which cf. Parisot in his *Praefatio*, sec. 17, ch. III. pp. lviii ff.

[3] *Sanh*, 97[a], cf. also *Rosh Hash.* 31[a], & Bacher, *Hag. d. Babyl. Amor.* p. 71 lix.

[4] Cf. O. Braun, *Beiträge zur Geschichte der Eschatologie in den syrischen Kirchen*, ZKTh. 1892 (col. 16) pp. 273—312

(*H. E.* iii. 39) in the Epistle of Barnabas,[1] and in many Christian
Apocryphal and Pseudepigraphical writings.[2] "Die Anschauung,
dass 1000 Jahre einem Tage vor Gott seien, war auf Grund der
Psalmstelle schon in vorchristlicher Zeit bei den Juden verbreitet,
und es wurden rabbinische Berechnungen angestellt".[3] St. Iranaeus
says that "in as many days as the world was made, in as many
years will it be ended".[4] He represents the early Christian theology which had "adopted the whole Jewish eschatology, the only
difference being that he regards the Church as the seed of
Abraham . . . . Wherever philosophical theology had not yet made
its way, the chiliastic hopes were not only cherished . . . . but
emphatically regarded as Christianity itself".[5]

In innumerable concrete instances of exact parallels in thought,
as well as in his general envisagement of theological problems,
we find that Aphraates is a "docile pupil of the Jews". In his
account of Creation, sin, and the Fall, the problems of salvation,
and redemption, his eschatology and his chiliasm, Aphraates is
peculiarly at one, in the idiom of his thought and the perspective
of his field, with contemporary Rabbinic Judaism. Where he
diverged, he only recombined elements taken from the Rabbis
to reassemble them into the contour of a mosaic of a Christian
character.

4. Aphraates and the *Didache*.

Schwen,[6] and Bert[7] both suggest the strong resemblance to be
found between the words of Aphraates in the so-called "Creed"

---

[1] xvi.4 of the Epistle; cf. *Barnabae epistola, graece et latine* . . . . Gebhardt und
Harnack, Leipzig, 1878, where (pp. 64—65 ff.) Harnack presents all the evidence,
parallel passages, etc.

[2] *F. g.*, W. E. Barnes, *Extracts from the Testament of Isaac*, appended to *Testament of Abraham*, ed. *James*, in *Texts and Studies*, vol. II., 2, pp. 140—151;
Visio Pauli (T. & S. ii. 3) chapter 21; cf. E. C. Dewick, *Primitive Christian Eschatology*, Cambridge, 1912, pp. 315—338.

[3] *Pistis Sophia*, ed. A. Harnack, in *T. u. U.*, vii Band, Heft 2, Leipzig, 1891, p. 22.

[4] *Adv. Haer.*, V. 28, 3.

[5] A. Harnack, *Dogmengeschichte*. (Engl. trans. vol. II. pp. 298—299).

[6] *Afrahat, Seine Person und sein Verständniss des Christentums.*—Berlin, 1907, p.65.

[7] *Afrahat's des persischen weisen Homilien. T.u.U. III*, Heft 3 and 4, p. 18, n. 1;
p. 19, n. 2.

at the beginning of the *Homilies*, and the *Didache*. Bert suggests the comparison between Aph. 44:21—26, 45:1—6; Lev. 19 [26], Deut. 18 [18], and *Did.* 3 [4]. The words in the *Didache*, "thou shalt not blaspheme, thou shalt not bear false witness, thou shalt be neither double-minded, nor double-tongued, for the double tongue (is guilty) of death",[1] are strikingly like those of Aphraates: "Withhold thyself from blasphemy; thou shalt not bear false witness, thou shalt not speak . . . with a double tongue".[2] On such passages Schwen comments that "they doubtless go back to an original common Jewish source".[3] Instances of similar dependence are well illustrated in certain other passages. In *Homily* IV. 'On Prayer' Aphraates comments on St. Matt. 18 [20]:[4]— "Where two or three are gathered together in My name, there am I in the midst of them." He goes on to say:[5] "How, beloved, dost thou understand these words? . . . if thou art alone, is not Christ with thee? It is written concerning believers in Him that Christ dwells with them.[6] By this (text) it is shown that when two or three are gathered together Christ is with them. I shall show thee that it is possible for not only two or three, but even for a thousand to be gathered together in the name of Christ, and yet for Christ not to be with them, while even one only may have Christ with him . . . . ." Then, after quoting the text again, he says,[7]—(in proof that a single individual may have Christ with him)—"When a man gathers himself in Christ's name, Christ dwells in him; and God dwells in Christ,—thus the (single) man becomes one from three,—himself and Christ Who dwells in him, and God who is in Christ, as our Lord Himself said:[8] 'I am in the Father, and the Father in Me', and (He said) 'I and the Father are One'.[9] Again He said:[10] 'Ye are in Me and I in you'. And again He said by the prophet:[11] 'I shall dwell in them and walk amongst them'. By this train of thought canst thou understand that word which our Saviour spake".

---

[1] *Did.* 23, 4.
[3] *Op. et pag. cit.*
[5] 161 : 1—10.
[7] 161 : 13—23.
[10] St Jn. 14 [20].

[2] 44:21, 26; 45:1—2.
[4] 160:22—26.
[6] I St. John 3 [24], etc.
[8] St. John 14 [10], [11].
[11] Lev. 26 [12], etc.

[9] St. Jn. 10 [30].

There is a very interesting text in the Oxyrhynchus Logia, no. 5[a], which reads as follows: λέγει Ἰησοῦς, Ὅπου ἐὰν ὦσιν β' οὐκ εἰσὶν ἄθεοι, καὶ ὅπου εἷς ἐστιν μόνος λέγω Ἐγώ εἰμι μετ' αὐτοῦ . . .[1]

"The meaning must be either, 'Wherever all are unbelievers and one alone is faithful, there am I with him', or, 'wherever there are two disciples I am with them, and wherever one is alone, I am with him . . . .' The two paralled clauses . . . . support the second alternative (Heinrici) and the passages from Clem. Alex., Strom. iii. 10, and Eph. Syr., Evang., cum. Exp. 14, decide almost certainly for the second view . . . . We have provisionally adopted the brilliant conjecture of Blass . . . 'Wherever there are two, they are not without God's presence, and if anywhere one is alone, I say I am with him . . . . .' It has been suggested that ἄθεοι[2] may be an allusion to the pagan nickname, 'they are not, as men call them, ἄθεοι, godless, etc."[3] This is Lock's interpretation of the text, and seems quite satisfactory. It is interesting that the commentary attributed to Eph. Syr. is extraordinarily like that which Aphraates says, though there is no literal agreement. According to the Latin translation of Mosinger[4] from the Armenian recension, the text runs: "Christus . . . . vitam solitariam agentes in hac tristi conditione consolatus est dicens: 'Ubi unus est, ibi et ego sum.' Ne quisquam ex solitariis contristaretur: . . . 'Et ubi duo sunt, ibi et ego ero',—quia misericordia et gratia ejus nobis adumbrat. Et quando tres sumus, quasi in ecclesia coimus, quae est corpus Christi perfectum, . ." etc. Taylor[5] quotes several passages in Pirke Aboth, Tal. Babli., Berach 6[a], which show Jewish

---

[1] C. Taylor, *The Oxyrhynchus Sayings of Jesus, found in 1903*,—Oxford, pp. 26—27.

[2] For ἄθεοι cf. Eph. 2 [11]. Harnack (in *Agrapha*, Resch, in *T. u. U.*, Band 5, Heft 4, Leipzig, 1889. p. 21, note) says: "In dem Evangelium aus welchen unser Spruch stammt, Gott und Christus sich besonders nahe gerückt waren."

[3] W. Lock, and W. Sanday, *Two Lectures on the Sayings of Jesus*,—Oxford, 1897, pp. 22—23.

[4] Quoted in Resch, *Agrapha*: T. u. U.. Band 5, Heft 4, pp. 295—296. (Leipzig 1889). He refers to Ign. *ad Eph.* v [2], and *Ps. Ign.* v, etc.; numerous parallels between Aph. and Eph. Syr. are noted by Parisot,—intro. pp. L—LL.

[5] C. Taylor, *The Oxyrhynchus Logia, and the Apocryphal Gospels*,—(Oxford, 1899) (cf. pp. 34—53).

affiliations with this notion. In Jewish tradition, the Shechinah abides over those who occupy themselves with the study of the Torah, one authority adducing the text Ex. 20 ²²⁻²⁵ ("In every place where I record my name, I shall come to thee"). There is a pun on the meaning of נוי in *Mid. Debarim Rab.* (2 ¹⁶) when 'God is said to be so near to him' (אליו—Deut. 4 ⁷); the text refers it to the people who were in such close proximity to God, the allusion here to the individual. Thus the meaning of *Didache* 4 ¹: ὅθεν γὰρ ἡ κυριότης λαλεῖται, ἐκεῖ κύριος ἐστιν[1] exactly agrees with a favorite principle of the Jewish Fathers that those who occupy themselves with words of the Torah .. have the Shechinah among them. The resemblance can be seen from the words of Rabin b. R. Ada in the name of R. Isaac: . . . 'God is in the synagogue with the מנין, since: 'God stands in the congregation of God . .'[2] מנין שהקב״ה מצוי בבית הכנסת שנאמר אלהים נצב בעדת אל ומנין לעשרה שמתפללין שכינה עמהם שני אלהים ונ' ומנין לשלשה שיושבין בדין ששכינה עמהם שנאמר בקרב אלהים ישפוט ומנין לשנים שיושבין ועוסקין בתורה ששכינה עמהם שנאמר אז נדברו יראי ה' איש אל רעהו ויקשבה ה' ונ' (Mal. 3 ¹⁶—cf. Ber. 6ª) and so on, basing the reason of the abiding of the Shechinah in one single person on the text of Ex. 20 ²¹. The handling of texts in Aphraates is conspicuously Jewish, and so are the ideas with which he deals, though the actual words of his text are from the N. T.

It seems rather extraordinary that one whole homily out of the 23 of Aphraates, should be devoted to the duty of almsgiving. Two facts, however, will make this appear not so strange. a) Our author is not concerned with abstract doctrines or teachings, but is devoting his energies to an exposition of the works which must accompany true faith and of the practical difficulties of the communities and Churches of his day. b) Our author is writing for monks, and one of the counsels which they had undertaken to follow as their life principle, was poverty. Consequently the duty of almsgiving assumed rather important proportions in his perspective. It was at once the practical exemplification of true

---

[1] C. Taylor, *The Teaching of the Twelve Apostles*, 1886. pp. 37—38.
[2] Ps. 82 ¹.

religion and an act of religion itself, in that its offices were wrought on the very person of Christ. I have no doubt that back of this double purpose lay a still more fundamental consideration in Aphraates' convictions; (for his convictions were unconsciously or consciously the result of Jewish tradition and training in relation to the view-point from which he envisages religion, and the atmosphere with which he invests it). He begins his "homily on the sustaining of the poor" with the words: "It is a great and praiseworthy gift, when it happens that a prudent man is able to give to the poor of the toil of his hands . . ."[1] He goes on to show the importance of the duty in the Torah, its place in the life of David, and finally cites the words of Christ,— St. Matt. 25 [32—45]—, where He identifies Himself with the poor to whom the ministration is offered. He then interprets the parable of the rich man and Lazarus,[2] allegorizing it in a thoroughgoing way: Christ is the poor man, the Gentiles the dogs who licked his sores, etc. Almsgiving, he shows from Dan. 4 [27], does away with sin, among its other valuable properties, as well as "sows the seed of (eternal) life."[3] Incidentally the state of poverty, being most like that of Christ, is to be preferred.[4]

While Aphraates nowhere expressly refers to toil as the curse laid upon man, his emphasis upon almsgiving as man's act in giving of the fruit of his toil,—which he obtains from the ground only at the price of his sweat and labor,—indicates in part that which may have been back of his thought. Almsgiving had a very large part to play in Jewish religious practice. "Whosoever 'shears' himself of his possessions and gives alms of them, escapes the condemnation of hell."[5] "Alms (צדקה) delivereth from death" (Prov. 11 [4]). This deliverance. according to *Bab. Bath.* 10[a], "frees one from the judgment of Gehinnom". According to Rabbi Eleazer, following Ps. 21 [3]: "He who does alms is greater than (he who offers) all sacrifices."[6] Rabbi Isaac's list of the four

---

[1] 893 : 1—3.   [2] St. Lk. 16 [19-31].
[3] 913 : 6—8; 929 : 3—4.
[4] *Homily* XX §§ 5—8.
[5] *Nah.* 1 [12].
[6] *Succah* 49 [6].

things which annul the judical sentence against man, puts alms-giving first.[1]

While there are ten things created, each one stronger than, and prevailing over the preceding, death being stronger than all together, alms delivereth from death.[2] Aphraates states that almsgiving is one of those good acts which refresh God.[3] "When a man gives of his substance to the poor he refreshes the will of God ܠܨܒ܏ ܐܠܗܐ and of Christ, as it is said: 'this is my refreshment: give the weary rest.'"[4] It is more important than prayer to Aphraates: "Beware, beloved, when some opportunity present itself (to thee) to refresh the will of God, lest thou say: 'the time of prayer is at hand: I shall pray, and afterward do this.' Before thou shalt have finished, that opportunity will have passed."[5] Prayer is better than sacrifices, since, as Aphraates says, it has supplanted them,[6] and prayer has become, together with fasting, the real sacrifice.[7]

The words in Aphraates:[8] a prudent man: ܓܒܪܐ ܚܟܝܡܐ are much like those in *Did*:[9] παντὶ τῷ αἰτοῦντί σε δίδου καὶ μὴ ἀπαίτει. πᾶσι γὰρ θέλει διδόσθαι ὁ πατὴρ ἐκ τῶν ἰδίων χαρισμάτων. μακάριος ὁ δίδους κατὰ τὴν ἐντολήν..... ἀλλὰ καὶ περὶ τούτου δὲ εἴρηται· ἱδρωσάτω ἡ ἐλεημοσύνη σου εἰς τὰς χεῖράς σου, μέχρις ἂν γνῷς τίνι δῷς... κ. τ. λ.

This passage in the *Didache* has a parallel in the *Sibylline Books* (ii. 77); and "the parallelism (of the *Sibylline Books*) with the language of the *Teaching* shows that in the latter the main idea is the connexion between personal charity and one's earnings."[10]

There is an interesting parallel to the passages, among others

[1] *Rosh Hash.* 16ᵇ.
[2] *Bab. Bath.* 10ᵃ.
[3] 920 : 12—16.
[4] Is. 28 ¹².
[5] 172 : 6—14.
[6] 181 : 16—18.
[7] 245 : 19—20.
[8] 893 : 2—3.
[9] From Text, in C. Taylor, *Essay on the Theology of the Didache* (Cambridge, 1889.) p. 140.
[10] J. Rendel Harris, *Teaching of the Apostles and the Sibylline Books*, (Cambridge, 1885) pp. 7—8.

quoted by Taylor:[1] καὶ ἄλλος πάλιν ὁ μισϑὸς τοῦ γεωπόνου ἐξ ἰδίου ἰδρῶτος ποιοῦντος συμπάϑειαν, καὶ ἕτερος ὁ τοῦ ἄρχοντος τοῦ ἀπὸ δώρων καὶ πρωσώδων παρέχοντος. The parallel passages in the 'Shepherd', the Apostolic Constitutions, etc., are given, loc. cit.

It is in his explanation[2] of the words of the Did. 16[5b]: "σωϑήσονται ὑπ' αὐτοῦ τοῦ καταϑέματος" that Harris coins the phrase 'salvation by similars' to distinguish that type of 'popular canon of soteriology.' "The antidote", he says,[3] "grows on the same stem with the poison: that which damns turns into that which saves." To illustrate his point, he suggests that the meaning of the text of St. Jn. 3[14] ("as Moses lifted up" etc.) is clear when the change of the word נחש into משיח by "gematria" is kept in mind. "In this way man is saved by the very curse itself."[4] Harris adduces a number of references bearing out his contention,—Severianus of Gabala in Jewish controversy, Ireaneus, etc. In the N. T. this usage is not unfamiliar,—"as in Adam all die, so in Christ shall all be made alive."[5] Christ is the Second Adam,[6] and through Him life is restored, after the first Adam had brought death. That "through him He might destroy him that had the power of death, the devil," was the purpose of Christ's coming.[7] According to Aphraates,[8] the Incarnation was a necessity in order to give God a way to come at death. It was by the body man had sinned and incurred death: by the body must be made the conquest of death. Death, sin, the curse,[9] and the easy access of the devil to man came through Eve.[10] "Through the coming of the Son of Mary the thorns are uprooted, the sweat wiped away, ... dust becomes salt,"[11] "the

---

[1] Cf. Ps. Athan., J. R. Harris, Questiones ad Antiochum duc., in Teaching of the Apostles, pp. 15—16 (Baltimore, 1887.)

[2] Ibid., p. 62 (Text, p. 10).

[3] p. 62; cf. Just. Trypho: ὁ Νῶε ἐν ξύλῳ διεσώϑη, but the Fall had come by the tree, etc., (E. Archambault, Textes et documents, p. 296, col. 2).

[4] p. 63 ibid.   [5] I Cor. 15[22-23].

[6] Ibid 41-49; cf. Aph. 307 : 14, &ff.

[7] Harris, op. cit., p. 66.

[8] II. 32 : 9—16.   [9] 265 : 3—11.

[10] 265 : 15—18.

[11] Cf. the curse of Adam in Gen.; an antidote for the Devil is salt, since he cannot eat it; cf. Gen. 3 [11b], [20b], Aphr. 256 : 5—6.

curse is affixed to the cross," etc. For further parallels to this, cf. J. Rendel Harris, op. cit., pp. 66—67.

This, according to Harris, is the significance of almsgiving in Jewish tradition: it is 'the pains God gives man for his salvation.' It may be, too, that this lay in the background of Aphraates mind. It is quite clear that he conceived of there being a potential blessing in the act of the eating from the tree,[1] though the act incurred a curse on man. Those who had eaten of the fruit of the tree had the principle of life preserved in themselves, and "they received in their bodies the abrogation of the curse."[2] The sentence passed upon the serpent was, according to Rab. Eleazer, both a blessing and a curse, for a blessing was involved in the curse:[3] ‏אף קללת של הקב"ה יש בה ברכה‎. The same notion of 'salvation by similars' appears in Aphraates:[4] "The blood of Christ . . . . . it is which stained them, and they were not able to be clean of it. But if they were washed in the water of baptism, and received the Body and Blood of Christ, blood would be expiated by the Blood, and body cleansed by the Body . . ."

Harris suggests other conspicuously Jewish features in the *Didache*, to which we find parallels in Aphraates. Thus the careful precepts about fasting for the Neophyte[5] and about his baptism, according to Harris indicates a Jewish original. Aphraates calls fasting and prayer, "desirable fruits," "a (worthy) sacrifice to be offered to the King." Rab. Shesheth, a little before the time of Aphraates, is quoted by Harris to show that fasting took the place of the sacrifice which had ceased to be offered. Aphraates devotes one homily to the subject of fasting, and places it between love and prayer. He considers it as an offering made to God, and adds that it must proceed from true religion, and one rightly ordered ethically: the fast of the Marcionites, Valentinians, and the like, is inacceptable to God.[7] A sinner's fast

---

[1] xxiii, section 3.   [2] II. 8 : 15.
[3] *Mid. Ber. R.* 20 [8].
[4] 181 : 7—14, and cf. 981 : 11—13.
[5] *Didache* VII. 4 and cf. Aph. *Hom.* III; 245 : 19—20.
[6] On p. 88. *op. cit.*, cf. *Berach*, 17 [a].   [7] Cf. iii., section 9.

destroys its own value.[1] Fasting of the true sort involves much more than a simple abstinence from food.[2]

The method of interpretation of the O. T. in the Didache is expressed in these words: "πᾶς δὲ προφήτης δὲ δοκιμασμένος, ἀληθινός, ποιῶν εἰς μυστήριον κοσμικὸν ἐκκλησίας, μὴ διδάσκειν δὲ ποιεῖν ὅσα αὐτὸς ποιεῖ, οὐ κριθήσεται ἐφ' ὑμῶν. κ. τ. λ.

Taylor discusses this at length,[3] and adduces very interesting illustrations and interpretations of his explanation of the passage. He finds that 'the Teaching' interprets the O. T. in the manner of Barnabas and Justin Martyr, seeing in it everywhere a πρᾶξις εἰς μυστήριον τοῦ Χριστοῦ. This principle is applied incidentally in justification of unusual conduct in the Christian prophets, but it is not to be limited to acts which stand in need of apology.[4] "This 'unusual conduct' must proceed however from an intention to perform such abnormal actions with symbolic reference to the Church and its affairs." Harris says[5] that this sort of action, 'not to be imitated, was only done to expound some mystery.' This μυστήριον κοσμικόν is the Rabbinic כבשונו של עולם. Such actions were the making of the brazen serpent by Moses, (Num. 21 [8—9]) in flat contradiction to the Second Commandment,[6] Jacob's marriage of four women, and in Irenaeus (IV. xx. 12) Hosea's fallen wife, and the like. Thus St. Paul speaks of a woman being sanctified by a faithful husband, and St. Irenaeus says: *Id quod a propheta typice per operationem factum est, ostendit apostolus vere factum in ecclesia a Christo.*[7] So also the marriage of Moses is a type of that of the Church and Christ.

Aphraates in Homily xviii is presenting the subject of celibacy and the dedicated life to the Jews. After adducing as many scriptural illustrations as possible, (which, so far as his literal

---

1 113:13—14.
2 97:7—9.
3 In *Theology of the Did.*, p. 156.
4 Taylor, *op. cit.*, p. 150, ibid.
5 *Op. cit.*, p. 72.
6 Cf. Justin, *Trypho.*, ed. Arch., 2 p. 280 (134:1—2).
7 Cf. St. John Chrysostom's *Synopsis*; St. Athanasius, *De virginitate*, section 2, (Taylor, *op. cit.*, p. 151).

proof of Divine sanction to a dedicated life of continence in
the O. T. is concerned, do not apply), he concludes his homily
with the words: "And this lot entails a great reward, since we
accept it voluntarily and not in obedience to a command, nor
by the necessity of (obeying) an injunction, nor are we bound
to it under the Law. We may find the type and the likeness
of it in the Scriptures, and may see in those who have conquered, the likeness of the Angels of heaven, (realized) by a
special gift (of God) on earth . . ."[1] It may be noted incidentally
that the reference here and in the passage quoted above, "who
will recompense the fasting of Valentinus, will reward Marcion,"[2]
is suggestive of the ideas associated with the doctrine of the
"two ways" in the *Didache*. The passage is collated with the
Targum by Harris,[3] who points out several passages allied to
the words of the *Did.* iv. 7: "γνώσῃ γὰρ τίς ἐστιν ὁ τοῦ μισθοῦ
καλὸς ἀνταποδότης." He concludes: "Whatever may be thought
of this parallelism it can hardly fail to be regarded as a striking
Hebraism on the part of the *Teaching*."[4]

5. Aphraates' use of the Scriptures.

A still more interesting question with regard to the *Homilies* is
Aphraates' use of the Bible, his method of quotation, style, and
interpretation of biblical passages. His view of the Bible and of
the necessity for a living tradition do not surprise us, in view of
his remarkably Jewish affiliations in other respects. He usually
quotes the writer of the passage by name, if possible, though he
often uses the ordinary Jewish word כתיב. Schwen[5] notes that
Bewer[5] finds 86 occasions of the use of this word in Aphraates
in connection with the O. T. and 19 with the N. T. He usually

---

[1] 84! : 19—25.
[2] 116 : 6— 17.
[3] *Op. cit.*, p. 78.
[4] *Ibid.* p. 79.
[5] *Op. cit.*, pp. 30 ff.
[6] *The History of the N. T. Canon in the Syriac Church*, in *A. J. T.*, 1900,
pp. 64 f.; 345 ff.

calls it "the Scripture" (ܟܬܒܐ). At times he quotes the prophets
as mouth-pieces of God, who speak His words in the first person.
God speaks through the Holy Scriptures,[1] and His Spirit was
upon the prophets.[2] For Aphraates the O. T. was an objective
unity, and possessed Divine authority.[3] Aphraates delights to
find parallels and "types." Thus Gideon's act was the presentation
in figure of something yet to come,[4] for it was the great mystery
of Baptism which he prefigured[5] and foreshadowed as a "typos".
He frequently develops parallels in word, act, general configuration,
and concrete detail, between Jesus Christ and the O. T. worthies.
This method of presentation comprises the greater part of the
content of his homily 'on Persecution.'[6] He employs the word
ܪܡܙ to express "foreshadowing," together with ܫܡܠܐ to denote "fulfilment." As with type in prophecy and realization in fact, so
with life, action, and word in symbolic meaning in the Old, and
with completion in deed in the New Dispensation. "Thou hast
heard," he says in his homily on the Passover,[7] "of that passover
of which I told thee that it was given to the former people
(ܠܥܡܐ ܩܕܡܝܐ) as a mystery (ܐܪܙܐ) and that its truth is today made
known among the Gentiles."

There is much that is Jewish in his method of approach to the
Scriptures, yet the characteristic and fundamental Christocentric
point of view of our author must not be obscured. All of the
furniture of his illustrations and imagery, all of his sources and
texts, are Biblical, and his manipulation of them is in the main
in accord with Jewish methods; his conclusions only are different.
His method of interpretation of the text,—to find a deeper and
more significant meaning behind the words than is conveyed on
their surface,—may well be compared to the process of interpretation in Jewish tradition. For example, Aphraates speaks[8] of

[1] 749 : 3—4.
[2] 752 : 22 etc.
[3] Cf. Schwen, op. cit., p. 35.
[4] 344 : 10—11.
[5] 344 : 22—23.
[6] No. xxi. sections 8—20.
[7] 516 : 3—5.
[8] 508 : 22.

the "great and wondrous mysteries" brought forth by the account
of the Passover in Ex. 12 44-45. The תושב and שכיר are nothing
else than the "(followers of) the teachings of the Evil One who
are not permitted to eat of the Passover."[1] So again, circumcision
was only a type and symbol of the true circumcision, which is
baptism.[2] There is an occasional lapse into the allegorical method
of interpretation, but it has developed nothing of the proportions
to which, for example, Clem. of Alex. developed it. On the other
hand, Aphraates was not tied down to the historico-grammatical
method of the[3] Antiochene School. He was strongly antiadop-
tionistic and his strong theological antipathy may account for
his rejection of the characteristically Antiochene method of
exegesis. The Bible was practically his sole authority and he
knew the contents as few men have. While the idiom of his
thought was Jewish, his combination of various elements and the
resulting teaching were quite his own. The Bible was interpreted
in accordance with a living tradition,[4] and Aphraates claims that
his own ܐܬܘܚܐ were not written according to any single individual's
private opinion, nor necessarily for the purpose of any single
person's needs whom he might have had in mind,[5] but in accord
with the mind of the whole Church, and for the exposition of
the faith in its general aspects.[6]

Bacher translates the words דברים בנו, attributed to R. Karna,
contemporary of Rab. (175—247)[7]: "Herein ist ein Geheimnis
verborgen."[8] With this may be compared the two methods of
interpretation,—the one proceeding from the simple and obvious
meaning of a word, phrase, or passage in its context, and
according to the rules of grammar,—the פשט, and the more
artificial interpretation,—the דרש.[9] The result of this latter type

[1] 525 : 10—12.
[2] Cf. XI section 11.
[3] Cf. L. Pirot, L'oeuvre exégétique de Théodore de Mopsueste, Rome, 1913, pp. 10—23.
[4] 1045 : 13—14.
[5] 1044 : 25—27.
[6] 1045 : 1—2.
[7] Mielziner, Intro. to Talmud, p. 43.
[8] Die Hag. der Amoräer, p. 37 note 7. cf. Ketuboth III a; Kid. 44 b.
[9] "פשטיה וקרא", in Ḥullin 6a; cf. R. Kahana, in Sab. 63a.

of interpretation is termed *Midrash*, of which there came to be
developed two kinds, "midrash halacha," legal, and "midrash
(h)aggada", homiletic.   Back of the plain meaning may lie,
according to Rabbinic tradition, an esoteric signification, deep
and hidden, the סוד. Acquaintance with the elaboration and
articulation of the rules of interpretation into a code (under Rabbi
Išmael, who rejected much of the fanciful method evolved by
R. Akiba) is nowhere apparent in the writings of Aphraates. He
simply regarded the Bible as the Word of God,[1] divinely inspired by the Holy Spirit speaking through the individual writers,[2]
beneath every word of which lay a hidden meaning, to be
ascertained by reverent allegorization or mystical application.

It is not difficult to show that Aphraates' attitude towards
the study of the Scriptures resembles that of the Jews of his
day to the study of the Torah. Its study was the end for which
man was created, and he ought not be proud of having done
that for which he was brought into the world.[3] He should be
prepared to suffer anything for its sake. In such a one, according
to R. Jose b. R. Hanina, the words of the Torah abide, and,
according to R. Johanan, in a man who because of his great
humility regards himself as naught. The necessity of this humility
in the student of the Scriptures is emphasized by Aphraates in
homily xxii, section 26. The "Holy Scriptures" (כתבי קדש) in
Aphraates ܟܬܒܐ ܩܕܝܫܐ[4] were inspired by God, and His Spirit spake
through patriarchs and prophets. The Spirit,[5] according to Gen. 1 [2]
of the Targum Onkelos, is רוחא מן קדם and was created on the
first day, as one of the ten things[6] then brought into existence.
According to Jewish tradition it rested upon the Patriarchs, and
this same Spirit was in the Scriptures,[7]—the רוח נבואה which spake,
inspired, and prophecied. As has been shown, the "Spirit",—called

----

[1] 756:1, 12, etc.

[2] 328:8; 405 13.

[3] From *Aboth de R. Nathan*, ed. Schechter p. 58, note 5, and cf. the words of
R. Jose bar Chanina on Prov. 8 [12], in *Sota* 21 [b].

[4] 1045:18.

[5] 292:14.

[6] *Hagiga* 12 [a].

[7] Cf. Weber, *op. cit.*, p. 193.

the "Holy Spirit", "or Spirit of Christ", or "the Spirit" in Aphraates,— has all of these same functions attributed to it, save that it is nowhere stated that it was created by God. The Spirit of God had inspired the Holy Scriptures and thus they became utterly different from ordinary human writings.

The individual could appropriate as much of their meaning as he could use and stood in need of,—but could never exhaust them. The content of the Scriptures is infinite. "If thou hast received of the Spirit of Christ, Christ suffers no loss, and if Christ abide in thee, yet He is not confined to thee."[1] Then after illustrating his meaning with the figure of the sun, he says: "thereby know thou that the word of God no man has compassed, nor has he set a bound to it."[2] With the Jewish quotation noted above (that it is the duty of a man to study the Torah, since for that purpose he was created), it is interesting to compare the following words of Aphraates, at the end of his 22nd homily: "I have written these words .... a man born of Adam, molded by the hands of God, a student (ܬܠܡܝܕܐ) of the Holy Scriptures."[3] His own characterization of himself was as a human being, in whose creating God had exercised his infinite care, and whose essential function lay in being a student of God's word. A cursory glance at the text of Aphraates would convince anyone that his questioner[4] did not err in attributing to him power of exposition of Holy Scripture.

Aphraates' saying that so infinite was the depth of Holy Scripture that were a man to study constantly from the time of Adam till the end of the world, he could not exhaust or fathom the meaning of it, (since no one can comprehend the wisdom of God)[5] is much like the words of R. Eleazar, quoted in *Shir Rabba*: ".....Were all the seas ink, and all the reeds pens, and heaven and earth books (מגלות) and all men writers, yet were they unable to write down the knowledge of the Law which I have obtained,

---

[1] 236 : 22—25.
[2] 237 : 2—4.
[3] 1049 : 1—4.
[4] 1 : 6—7.
[5] 1048 : 12—18.

and yet I have taken as little from it as a man who dips his pencil's point in the sea, from the water of the ocean." When Aphraates says "the Word of God is like a pearl which reveals new beauties with each new aspect of it," his thought is reminiscent of the words of the school of Rabbi Ismael on Jer. 23 [29]: "As a hammer breaks a rock, as (the stone by) the hammer is shattered to bits, thus one single text issues in to a number of interpretations."[1]

In another place Aphraates compares the Holy Scriptures to the water which quenches the thirst of the Gentiles. Commenting on Is. 41 [17−19], he says:[2] "Thus does God take care of the needy .... because their tongue was dried up for the lack of water: (he says) 'I shall open rivers in the mountains,'[3] .... The poor and needy who seek the water and have it not, are the people of the Gentiles; the water is the teaching of the Holy Scriptures...."[4] In *Mid. Shir. Hash:* "The words of the Torah are likened to water .... (as) water is not delightful to a man except he thirst for it, (so) the Torah is not delightful to him except he crave it."[5]

The Scriptures then objectively are universal and infinite in scope and content. Each must learn from tradition the interpretation of them, but is not limited thereto, according to Aphraates. There may be differences of opinion, yet "whoever reads the Holy Scriptures,—both the former and latter ones in both testaments,—and reads willing to be convinced, (ܠܡܐܣ) he can both learn and teach."[6] Aphraates believes that the product of such studies should be submitted to the whole body of the Church, to be ratified and corrected there, and should gain acceptance because of their intrinsic value under these conditions, and not because of the person of the author.[7]

A. M. D. G.

---

[1] *Sanh.* 34 9.   [2] 913 : 15—16.

[3] 913 : 18, 25—26.   [4] 916 : 1—2.

[5] *Mid. Shir. R.* 1 [19], and ff. So "the Scripture is likened to water, the *Mishna* to wine, the *Gemara* to spiced wine." The idea is, that water is of the greatest necessity to the slaking of thirst,—wine is excellent, but the spiced appetizing drink a luxury and available to only a few; from *Sopherin* 96.

[6] 1045 : 17—20; 1044 : 25—27; 1045 : 1—2.

[7] 1048 : 26.

VITA

I was born of Dr. William James Gavin and Laura Burns Gavin, in Cincinnati, Ohio, October 31, 1890. After attending the graded schools in that city, I graduated from Hughes High School, and entered the University of Cincinnati in 1907. At the beginning of the Junior year's work I became as well a regular student at the Hebrew Union College, and for part of a year took a special course at the Jesuit College of St. Francis Xavier. In 1912 I received the degree of B. A. from the University of Cincinnati, and in September entered the General Theological Seminary, New York. During the three years' course at the latter institution I enrolled as a Graduate Student at Columbia University, where I received the degree of Master of Arts in 1914, and became University Fellow, teaching in the department of Semitic Languages. In 1915 I was ordained to the priesthood in the Episcopal Church, and graduated from the General Seminary with the degree of Bachelor of Divinity. Having been appointed to a parish in Cincinnati, I was unable to accept the appointment as Gustav Gottheil Lecturer at Columbia. In October, 1916, I went to Boston, Massachusetts, to try my vocation in the Society of St. John the Evangelist, and was stationed at St. Francis House, Cambridge. Upon continuing my studies in the fields of Semitic and Early Christian Literature at Harvard University, I received in 1917 the degree of Master of Sacred Theology from the latter institution, and in 1919, that of Doctor of Theology. The year before, the Faculty of the Hebrew Union College made an exception in my case and did me the honor of conferring on me the degree of Bachelor of Hebrew Literature. During the year 1919—1920 I taught at Nashotah House, Nashotah, Wisconsin, a seminary for the training of priests of the Episcopal Church, and in 1920—1921 went to Greece to make a special study of the thought of present-day Greek Orthodoxy. The results are embodied in the Hale Lectures for 1922, "Some Aspects of Contemporary Greek Orthodox Thought", Morehouse Publishing Co., Milwaukee, Wisconsin, 1923, pp. xxxiv—430. On my return to America I withdrew from the Society of St. John the Evangelist, not having been admitted to life vows. In June (1921) I married Eula Christian Groenier, and the same month was elected to the chair of New Testament, Nashotah House, which I held until my election to that of Ecclesiastical History at the General Theological Seminary, New York (May 1923).

Bei Fragen zur Produktsicherheit wenden Sie sich bitte an:
If you have any questions regarding product safety,
please contact:

Walter de Gruyter GmbH
Genthiner Straße 13
10785 Berlin
productsafety@degruyterbrill.com